# Fearless Victor

Freedom from Anxiety by the
Leading of the Holy Spirit

By Chelsey Dollman

Title: Fearless Victor
Subtitle: Freedom from Anxiety by the Leading of the Holy
Spirit

Cover: All design elements are by the talented graphic
designer, artist and song writer, Alisha Kairos. Thank you for
honouring me with your gifts.

Cover photos: taken by Chelsey Dollman.

---

This book is dedicated to beloved husband who loves me
**fearlessly** and without fault. Who has walked through the
valleys with me, and by his joyful humour, has brought me up
to the mountain peaks. Life would be much less "everything"
without you.
I love you.

---

# Table of Contents

# *Introduction*

Whether you're a new Christian or have been a Christian your entire life, this book is for you. If you want to step out of the cycle and fear and follow the guidance of the Holy Spirit to lead you into freedom, this book is for you. God doesn't use the perfect, He uses the willing. Time after time, we see this principle in Scripture. I know that you are willing to do the work, otherwise you wouldn't have picked up this book.

My prayer is that you are encouraged to start this journey and do the work that you need to do, while in partnership with God doing what He is going to do in you. Together, as you co-labour with God, you will see the fruit of your hard work. I believe that God will give you the grace to overcome this obstacle because He is faithful to the very end.

He is faithful in big and in small ways. For example, you'll notice that the cover of this book, is photos of a collection of hearts. But they aren't generic stock photos, purchased to 'pretty up' the cover. They carry a personal story with them. What I'm about to share with you is so deeply intimate and personal that it brings me to tears as I write this.

When I began my journey of freedom from fear, by the leading of the Holy Spirit, I felt the love of God so close to me. I felt it with me everywhere I went, as it always is, but

I was so aware of His love and felt it so deeply. As I began the journey, I started noticing these 'heart' symbols were showing up in the oddest places. For example, I would be scrambling some eggs and a chunk of the egg would land on the pan in a heart. Or I'd be rinsing the sink and there in the basin would be a pile of bubbles in the shape of a heart. In fact, the middle photo in the top row, the heart is the centre of a sweet potato that I baked! I was astonished! At first I didn't recognize that it was a message God was giving me. But then all of the sudden, the Holy Spirit made me so keenly aware of these hearts. I felt the Holy Spirit telling me that it was a message of love from God. For me to reminded of His love for me in the midst of my day. Throughout the day. Sometimes the hearts were to distract me from negative thinking and sometimes they were there to as a reminder, to fill my mind with the love of God. Other times they would come when I was down and needing encouragement. And still other times, they would come when I had a moment of breakthrough and God was reminding me of His love in the victory over that battle. I can tell you that it's been the most tangible and profound blessing to me. During that journey, they were like angelic-visits that got me through the day. These photos were all taken by me, over the course of two years, but the amazing thing is that the hearts haven't stopped. This isn't even all of them, the cover could not contain them all, just like our hearts and minds cannot contain or understand all the love from our Father.

Why do I share this with you? Because I want you know that God is doing the same for you. It may be through supernatural hearts or it may be in other ways but He *is* showing His love for you! And I encourage you to keep your eyes and ears open to seeing the ways He is showing you His love. Ask the Holy Spirit to open your spiritual eyes and ears to see the Father's love. You will be blessed beyond measure.

I also tell you this because I want to encourage you that you don't need to only be in 'dedicated God-time' (ie: devotional time or in a closed room in prayer) for God to be at work in your life. He is active and at work all day long and all night, in you. He is working on your behalf to grow you 'little by little' (Deuteronomy 7:22) and 'day by day' (2 Corinthians 4:16). Know and think about how God is with you right now, all day long and ponder His presence in your life. Sometimes He uses a song, a Scripture, a friend, or a still, small voice to communicate that love to you, but it is there. Let Him interrupt your thoughts all day long. You are surrounded by the love of the King and He cannot wait to show up and show that to you. Enjoy the exciting adventure of being led by the Holy Spirit and seeing what amazing plans God has in store for you. He loves you so much and I pray that this book would bring you practical teachings that will propel you closer to God and lead you into a place of complete freedom!

*"The Lord bless you
and keep you;*

*the Lord make his face shine on you
and be gracious to you;*

*the Lord turn his face toward you
and give you peace."*

*Numbers 6:22-26*

# Chapter 1

---

## Walking the Journey

How many times have you felt out of control? Too many to count? If we serve a God who loves us so intensely, why should there even be a reason to worry? Well, really, there shouldn't be. Yet our human minds can sometimes get in the way of our spiritual ones. We ask ourselves questions like this and we worry we are lacking faith if we struggle with anxiety. I know the feelings you have, because I have had the very same ones. I lived so many wasted years in fear, worry and anxiety. I didn't even know what it was at the time, because I had grown so accustomed to my way of living. I had grown accustomed to the symptoms. Sweaty. Panic-stricken inside. Rapid heartbeat. Dizziness. Feeling like the fear is suffocating. Deep down, knowing that you're fears are irrational, yet somehow they're so very real to you. No one seems to understand how you feel because they don't struggle with the same crippling fear. They tell you not to be afraid and it seems simple to them. But the fear is often debilitating. It holds you back. It holds you in a prison cell of being afraid to step out in many areas. It holds you back from taking chances on things, even fun things. It holds you back from trying something new. It holds your loved ones back from enjoying the real you, enjoying new adventures with you and they want you to be free. They try to help you but they don't know what to do to help you. But there *is* hope.

We want to rely on the Holy Spirit to calm our fears and so often the Holy Spirit does, but there is also choice involved in the process. If we expect the Holy Spirit to wave a wand every time we feel anxious, we've not gained any ability in the matter. See, God is not the one giving us anxiety, it's our broken thoughts. Fear does not come from God, in any form. It says so right in 2 Timothy 1:7, "*For God has not given you a spirit of fear but of power, love and a sound mind.*" Instead, fear is typically a result of some painful experience or trauma in our past that gets us stuck in a thought pattern of fear. Then our mind gets stuck in a loop of replaying those thoughts over and over. And each time we replay those painful experiences or thoughts, our mind cannot separate whether its the past or present and we begin to relive those painful emotions all over again. This has been widely studied and proven through science. will link the article at the end of the book, citing the scientific evidence behind this phenomenon in the brain named neuroplasticity. Rather than just thinking about the past, you are reliving it when you keep thinking about it. This creates a powerful cycle of reoccurring emotional trauma and if you get stuck in the loop, that's what creates anxiety. It's not your fault in fact, it's your brain getting stuck in a loop. The good news is, you can retrain your brain's thought pattern, but we will explore that later.

Some of those negative thoughts are our own but most of those thoughts are lies planted by the enemy. When he first plants the seed, we may ignore it for a while or be unaware of it. But as that seed gets deeper roots, as we dwell upon the thoughts it produces, it goes from being a tiny seed to a well-established weed. A weed that begins to take over our thought process and before you know it, you're on a bunny trail that's led you down an emotionally destructive path. It can be overwhelming and feel completely real, even though it's not. Perceived reality and reality are two very different things but they can feel the same. Why is that? It's because our feelings lie.

But we have a choice in this. We can choose to believe the Word and what God says or we can choose to believe what we feel. But here's the kicker: the Word is true. And we just learned that our feelings can lie. So isn't the choice pretty clear?

Yes.

But is it as simple as that?

I wish.

Making a choice in your mind is hard to do. You are pushing against the natural grain of how you feel. There have been moments where I would wish my feelings weren't so strong, in the moments where I felt out of control of my feelings. But our feelings are there for a reason. There are times when they are very purposeful and useful. After all, God created them. They are in essence, what makes us humans and makes us alive. But when we let our feelings rule us, they're out of hierarchy with their purpose. *Our feelings are not meant to be our compass.* Yet sometimes, inevitably we let them.

Feelings are useful in many positive ways but they can also be unreliable and lie to us. We have to be standing guard on what we think about. Being aware of where our thoughts are at all times, because as Joyce Meyer's states, in her book *Battlefield of the Mind,* "the mind is the battlefield" where the enemy likes to do battle. He wants to win over your mind, but God has given us the armour to combat and win that battle. God also fights those battles for us because as it's written in 2 Chronicles 20:15, *"For the battle is not yours but God's.*" (NIV). You're not doing this alone. He is fighting powers and principalities for you when you surrender your heart to Him.

You also have a part though and it involves taking some purposeful steps. Steps like renewing your mind, casting your cares, submitting your thoughts, surrendering your agendas and choosing the believe the truth. That may sound like a lot but it's not because it involves your intention. Choosing these things and sticking to them is something you have to be willing to do. God will do His part and you must do your part. It will take practice and perseverance, but God will give you the ability, perseverance, guidance and courage to do it.

### Never give up
*"Because you know the truth, you don't have to be a slave to the lies."*

This was a revelation God downloaded to me one day. I don't even remember where I was when He told me, but I knew I needed to write it down. I *do* remember I was in a rush so I found a pen and quickly jotted it down in my devotion journal, and then had forgotten about it. One day, a few weeks later, I came across it. I realized I hadn't thought or prayed much about what God had said to me since I wrote it down. I began to ponder what it meant and why God had revealed it to me.

As I sat and thought and prayed about it, I felt God saying to me that He was telling me this in order that I would get a stirring in my heart to start to write this book, to help set those free who read it. And He wanted me to know that I didn't have to believe the lies the enemy was telling me. He had been downloading revelations about freedom from anxiety to me for months, and I was becoming more attuned to hearing and responding to His promptings. After all, God *is* truth. That's what He speaks and that's what He is. We serve Him because we love Him and He is such a good God. But we can easily become distracted with the lies we hear. And the thing is we don't even realize we are listening to the lies. There's a difference between hearing and listening. Hearing is a physical action- like you hear a bird singing.  But listening, that is a mental/ emotional action.

We begin by first hearing a lie, which pops into our mind as a thought, but we don't give it much weight. However, the enemy is persistent. He continues to whisper it to you, sneakily, and over time you start to pay attention to what this lie is telling you. Then you start to listen to the lie. You've gone from it being a common, human occurrence (such as a thought popping into your mind) to a now believing a lie that you didn't even realize was a lie. You don't even realize you've done this because it's often slow and sneaky. But before long, you're now believing a lie that the enemy has told you.

You've become a slave to your mind. And it happened while you weren't even paying attention. It's not as if you knowingly opened the door to sin and let the enemy sneak in. But he's been around a long time, and he knows our human nature. It's our human nature to rely on ourselves, and rely on our feelings. It's human nature to have thoughts pop into your head. It's human nature to believe our thoughts and feelings, even if they're not accurate. It's human nature to assume the worst much of the time. The enemy knows this and he uses it as tactics to trick you into believing his lies. I want to set you free from something for a moment: you are more than your circumstances. Even if you did something that got you to the place of fear that you are in right now, it's not the end and God has a way out for you. God has given us a passage in His Word that describes this very thing.

*"And remember, if you were a slave when the Lord called you, you are now free in the Lord." 1 Corinthians 7:22 (NLT)*

In Christ, because of His blood, sacrifice and resurrection, His atonement for our sins and because of the new life we have in Him, we are now free. Free from condemnation, free from eternal damnation, free to live the life God designed for us. Isn't that good news? He has a new plan and a new life for us! But when we believe the lies of the enemy, no matter how false they are, we are a slave to those lies. They control us-our thoughts, actions, plans, decisions, behaviour, attitude-so many things. We are not walking in the freedom Jesus died to give us, instead we are letting our feelings and emotions control us. Being under anyone's control-we would all agree-is not freedom. And the one who hates us the most and is most interested in bringing us down (Satan) is the one we are being a slave to when we believe His lies. That sounds pretty harsh, I know, but sometimes we have to hear the hard truth to see what a mess we've gotten ourselves into, to allow God to step in and walk us *out*. Freedom isn't something we can achieve on our own-we needed Christ's sacrifice in order to atone for it. In the same way, we need to rely on God to show us the way out of the traps of the lies of the enemy, into the freedom that God offers. Into truth. Into full surrender of our emotions.

But how?

# Chapter 2

## The Principles of Walking Free

There are six principles to walking in freedom and being freed from the heaviness and chains of anxiety, worry and fear. I believe that these six principles were a download from the Holy Spirit, to be implemented in your life. In saying that, I want you to recognize that these can **only** be done with the help of the Holy Spirit and that He's doing his part but you also have a part to do. Following these six principles will be your practice *and* your prayer. Pray about these and ask the Holy Spirit to help you grow in these each day.

**Prayer and petition:**

*"Do not be anxious about anything, but in every situation, by prayer and petition, with thanksgiving, present your requests to God. And the peace of God, which transcends all understanding, will guard your hearts and your minds in Christ Jesus." Philippians 4:6,7 (NIV)*

This verse. This verse should be the cornerstone of your prayers and memorized and written on your heart. This verse has such a special place in my heart because I clung onto this verse for life. This verse was always in my heart and spoken out loud because it is exactly what I was contending for. I encourage you to post it in your house, on your phone-anywhere you will see it and be reminded. Let the living Word of God breathe life into you daily.

**Faith:**
*Jesus replied, "Truly I tell you, if you have faith and do not doubt, not only can you do what was done to the fig tree, but also you can say to this mountain, 'Go, throw yourself into the sea,' and it will be done. If you believe, you will receive whatever you ask for in prayer." Matthew 21:21,22 (NIV)*

Think about this verse. Study it. God is saying that faith is the only thing we need in order to see the miracles of God. Learning to overcome anxiety and be free is a miracle. God wants this for you. Have faith and do not doubt, no matter what thoughts pop into your head to make you believe otherwise. The enemy will try to plant doubt in your mind but stand firm on the promises of God and do no waver. Learn the Scripture and keep reading and studying it, posting it around your house or anywhere you need to see it be reminded. Keep your faith strong and ask God to give you the gift of faith!

**Study God's Word:**
*Jesus answered, "It is written: 'Man shall not live on bread alone, but on every word that comes from the mouth of God.'" Matthew 4:4 (NIV).*
*"For the word of God is alive and active. Sharper than any double-edged sword, it penetrates even to dividing soul and spirit, joints and marrow; it judges the thoughts and attitudes of the heart." Hebrews 4:12 (NIV).*

The Word of God is our daily bread and our life. It is our portion. Do you know what that means? God has given us the portion which we need to have enough. God always gives us enough to keep going and get through. His Word is what we need to keep filling ourselves up with, in order that the truth that comes from reading the Word would be so foundational and rooted inside of us that it begins to come out of us. Rather than searching for a verse to draw strength from, it begins to flow out of you and you can begin to pray it over yourself with conviction and a deep knowing of the truth that it holds. I know for myself, the more I studied the Word, the more I believed the truth and the more it set me free. Jesus even says that exact thing in the Word, and it's one of the promises of God:

*Jesus said, "If you hold to my teaching, you are really my disciples. Then you will know the truth, and the truth will set you free." John 8:31-32 (NIV)*

And I can say with conviction that this has absolutely been my experience. I have learned to keep filling myself up with the Word of God and in that process, it really began to set me free. It became truth and knowledge rather than just text. I began to walk in those truths, which before, I had only read about.

**Learn about God's character:**
*"The Lord is not slow to fulfill his promise as some count slowness, but is patient toward you, not wishing that any should perish, but that all should reach repentance." 2 Peter 3:9 (ESV).*

There are so many verses and passages about the character of God. This is one of many but I encourage you to do a study of His Character. You don't need a fancy bible study or a theological book to read, you just need to start studying by looking up verses that describe who God is. You can begin by using a search engine online and typing in, 'The character of God verses.' It's not meant to be complicated. The Word is there and God will help guide you as well. Once you begin to see the qualities of God's character, and read more about how He loves his children and the plans He has for you, (see Jeremiah 29:11) you will begin to know deep within yourself just how much you can rely and trust in Him. It will build your faith in Him. It will build your trust in Him. It will encourage you to call out His promises for you and stand on His Word to be your guide in this journey.

Know who you are in Christ and remind yourself continually:

*"But whoever is united with the Lord is one with him in Spirit." 1 Corinthians 6:17 (NIV).*

*"So God created mankind in his own image, in the image of God he created them; male and female he created them." Genesis 1:27 (NIV).*

*(also see 1 Corinthians 12:27, 1 Peter 2:9, Galatians 3:27-28, 1 John 3:1-2)*

God has given us His name. We are now His children, accepted into His family and we carry the anointing, power, authority and blessing that He died to give us. What an amazing privilege it is…but don't let it go to waste. Learn about it, study who you are in Christ. I lived so many years of my Christian walk, not knowing who I am in Christ. I'm sure you've heard that saying before, yet have you stopped to really ask yourself the answer to that? Have you taken the time to study the Word? It wasn't until I dove into studying and really searching for the answer to that question, that I began to know what to declare. I am able to declare and ask for the things I am reading in God's word because I know that it is truth and that we can ask for these things in Jesus' name. It says so right in John 14:13-14, *"And I will do whatever you ask in my name, so that the*

*Father may be glorified in the Son. You may ask me for anything in my name, and I will do it." (NIV).* So get yourself full of the Word, rooted in the Word so that you know the truth and can speak it over yourself with conviction, knowing that what you are saying are the promises of God, therefore they are yours to claim.

## Getting to the root of it:

A very large part of the journey to freedom from anxiety, worry and fear is getting down to the root of the problem. Ask the Holy Spirit to expose and reveal to you where the root of the fear comes from. Depending on what the worry or fear is, this may be harder for some areas than others. If it involves any kind of abuse, you may want to enlist the help of Christian counsellor to walk you through it. But that being said, the Holy Spirit is the best counsellor you could ask for and even in the area that were painful for me, the Holy Spirit was so gentle in His exposure and He handled it in such a way that left me uplifted and not ashamed. I would call it my 'Holy Spirit counselling sessions,' and I would just simply sit down and pray, thanking God for what He is about to do and then ask the Holy Spirit to show me where the root of my fear came from in (fill in the blank) and wait on Him to show me. He was so gentle with me and able to show me in a way that I felt freed, not condemned. If you're afraid to even begin to ask the Holy Spirit for the root, you need to stop and ask yourself if you want to be free or a slave. If you want to be a slave to the worry and fear you live with, you won't have to be exposed to the truth but you will continue to live captive in your worry and fear. On the other hand, if you're ready and willing to do the work of letting the Holy Spirit reveal the root of the issue to you, then it's time to dive in. God will give you the ability to see the truth and be gentle with it. If you're not ready yet, you don't need to be afraid because

God will only show and reveal it to you when you're ready. His timing is perfect and he will wait until you're ready. Here are some verses to confirm that truth.

*"But those who hope in the LORD will renew their strength. They will soar on wings like eagles; they will run and not grow weary, they will walk and not be faint." Isaiah 40:31 (NIV)*

*"Trust in the Lord with all your heart and lean not on your own understanding; in all your ways submit to him, and he will make your paths straight." Proverbs 3:5-6 (NIV).*

*"The heart of man plans his way, but the Lord establishes his steps." Proverbs 16:9 (ESV).*

**Recognizing the enemy's lies:**
We have an enemy and he is always looking for ways to trip you up and cause you pain and agony. He knows what has worked in the past with you and he knows exactly which targets to hit. When we react to certain situations, he takes note of that and remembers that it is an area of weakness for you. We all have different weaknesses. But the devil uses that to his advantage and knows where exactly to attack you. His battle plan is to find out where you're weak, figure out what things steal your peace, figure out what things cause you to be hurt, upset or question your faith, and those are the exact areas he will test you in. He will tempt you lose your trust in God. He will tempt you to lose some of your faith in God. He will tempt you to question God's plan and God's will for you. He will tempt you to take the control back and to try to be in charge of yourself. He doesn't want you to rely and trust on God because he knows God has such amazing plans for you. The enemy wants you to start relying on yourself and that

is one of the biggest *lies* and *traps* that he can setup for you. Don't let him win that battle.

Instead, recognize that if you feel like the progress you've made is being questioned: it's the devil. Recognize that if you're feeling fearful and feeling that you want to take control back in an area (even if you convince yourself it's just a teensy-teensy bit of control): it's the devil. Recognize that if you're being tested in an area you've just gained some victory over and you're questioning going backwards: it's the devil. He won't stop and he will keep trying to whisper thoughts and lies to make you disbelieve everything you've just learned about the truth. It's not you- it's the devil. But don't let him win and don't revert back to the way you were acting before that victory because there's something you *can* do!

You're probably asking: 'how?' You may be saying to yourself, "That's great that you are saying I can have the victory but how? How can I move forward when right now I feel nothing but fear?" And believe me, I would ask those same things! When you're in the middle of feeling fear, the last thing you want to do or feel you *can* do, is step forward. You want to slink back and tip-toe your way into the shadows but that's exactly when you need to take self-control of your mind, and choose to step forward in faith. But I am telling you with everything that is in me: You CAN do it! Believe the truth! If I can do it, you can because God helps all who ask Him and that includes *you*. (see John 14:14)

I'll tell you how: that is the exact time for you to start declaring right away, all that you know to be true. In the Action Plan chapter, you will learn about creating your own declarations based on your specific fears but also based on Scripture. Take the tools that God has already given you such as the Word of God, and your declaration and prayer…and use them! That's why He's given them to you, to use! And remember in all things, God is fighting your battles for you if you surrender it to Him. That's an important part: surrendering it to Him. Take yourself out of the equation and remember that you "can do all things through Christ who gives you strength." (Philippians 4:13 (NIV)). Don't get back in the drivers seat because you feel afraid…that's not the answer. You already know that doesn't work because you've tried it and you got stuck in a pattern of fear and worry, which is what led you to seek help and seek to find freedom. This is your path to freedom. This is your answer. This is the good plan God has for you. Let Him be your driver and let Him be in control, despite how you feel.

Also remember that your feelings can lie and even though you may feel afraid at the moment, remember that the moment *will* pass. And you'll feel the elation of that victory. And you'll feel proud of yourself and thankful to God that He got you through it. Trust me in this. I speak of what I know because I speak of my own battle where I would feel a moment of fear when I was out of control and I considered reverting back to my old ways.

I specifically remember the moment when I got some upsetting news from a phone call, in an area that I really struggled with fear. I had about 2 minutes (which felt much longer) where I began to weigh all my feelings. *Should I be afraid? Maybe trusting in God is a good idea in theory but maybe I'm supposed to do something here. Maybe I should take back a little bit of control and I'll feel better.* But it only took 2 minutes of going down that road to let the Holy Spirit step in and remind me, "Was that old way of doing things making you feel any better?" And I instantly knew that the answer was, no. That old way of doing things was a pit of torment. Literally. That's the best way I can describe it. And God had been setting me free, more and more and I was feeling more and more free each day. I was learning to rely on Him more each and day and the Holy Spirit was speaking to me more each day and the victories over fear were far more plentiful than ever before. I realized at that moment that I had a choice. I could go back to my old ways and back to the pit of torment, or I could press on in *hope* that God was going to take care of this, just like he had taken care of everything else. I could ask the Holy Spirit for faith, and trust that God was in control and that I was giving this situation to Him. I said the words out of my mouth, "Lord, I give this to you," and I let it go. Right when I did that, I felt the fear that had been building up in me for 2 minutes, just dissipate and fade away. It was another test and another victory. It was the best feeling in the entire world because I felt the elation of the victor. Those battles still come but I have such a higher success rate than I used to and those moments of fear get shorter and shorter, and far less frequent. But I am never naive enough to say that I will never be challenged. I have a humble approach to these victories and know that they are only because of the power of God working in me, and I am grateful for each victory. I give thanks to God who is at work in me (and you!).

Last but not least, do the work and strategies I've outlined in the chapter titled, "Action Plan." Don't skip ahead to that chapter because that chapter will not make sense without the information in-between. The chapters in-between explain how the brain works and the importance of understanding that in order to complete the Action Plan steps.

I would also highly recommend Joyce Meyer's book, *Battlefield of the Mind*. It's a New York Times Best-Seller for a reason and it has helped so many people become free from the emotional and mental anguish so prevalent in today's society. Personally, it has helped me in more ways than I explain. It was the beginning to finding freedom from fear, for me. The profound revelation that I was exposed to in the book, was the very beginning of my journey to finding freedom from fear. I don't say this lightly or to dramatize anything, but it literally changed my life. I came to realize that I needed to pay attention to what I was letting in. I needed to pay attention to what I was thinking about, and dwelling on. I didn't realize how often I'd let my mind wander and God revealed to me that my mind had become a wilderness. I was letting it wander aimlessly in the wilderness and as such, it had become wild. Any little thought that would pop in my head, I would begin to think about-unknowingly-and dwell upon it. I wouldn't even recognize the fact that 30 mins had passed and I was thinking about how much someone didn't like me or recalling a painful situation from the past. I would play scenarios through my head-imagined ones that I invented in my mind-and waste time planning for these imagined scenarios that were so unlikely to ever happen. I would tally up an accumulation of days and weeks, wasting my time focusing on the negative things, worries, fears, lies-and I didn't even realize it.

The hard part about anxiety is that it creates fear-sometimes a deep rooted fear that has been a lie from 20 years ago that you chose to believe, and now that fear has affected you for 20 years in different ways. But God opened my eyes to see that many of those fears were just lies that I had believed years ago, that I had not taken to God. God will always tell us the truth. Even if it's the hard truth but, oh, He is *so, so* gentle with us. Why do we choose to believe the lies instead of the truth? Why do we choose to be a slave instead of free?

The throne room.

We forget to go to the Throne room first and foremost and talk to God. When fears come into my mind now, I am aware of them. I first recognize that it may be a lie. I then take that to God and ask Him to search my heart. I ask Him to reveal to me, the truth. 100% of the time, God shows me the truth. And that truth is never any part of the lie. He always tells me the truth-about who I am, what the lie is and how it's not true. That doesn't mean God doesn't convict us when there are things we need to change but He never condemns us. And He always is gentle with His loving correction. Even when there are things I am convicted of, God knows exactly how to go about it.

Every day, every moment, I am so blessed by God's love. He loves us so much that He won't leave us where we are. He is always working on us to be better versions of ourselves. Today in society, correction is viewed as a negative thing. People are so easily offended by everything it seems, especially correction. Yet, I am glad when God corrects me because I know He's doing it for my good. He doesn't want me to wallow in my pain, or my slavery, or my bad habits. He wants to shine the light on those weaknesses so that through His help, I can change and live a more whole life. Just like it says in Hebrews 12:11, *"No discipline seems pleasant at the time, but painful. Later on, however, it produces a harvest of righteousness and peace for those who have been trained by it."*

God desires for us to walk in freedom, not slavery and sometimes the way to walk out of that is together, hand in hand, and with the truth as our guide. The truth is honest and serves the purpose of showing us what to improve so that we can improve ourselves and live a better life.

# Chapter 3

---

## Entering the Rest
### (and discovering who you are in Christ)

What does that mean? Discovering who are you in Christ is truly the answer to who you are. Aside from that, it is all meaningless and just an exercise. Nothing more. Who are we living for? Who are we here for? I hope you know on some level that God has put you here on earth for a purpose. He sees us with such a different set of eyes. Because of that, it's the only opinion we should care about. He's the reason for any of this, our mere existence. But of course whose opinions do we get bogged down with instead?

**Friends**-Will they think you're a good friend? Will they approve of how your dress, or how you act? Do they truly love you for who you are?

**Neighbours**- Do they approve of how you take care of your yard/house? Do they think you're a good neighbour?

**Co-workers**- Do they think you're a good employee? Are they jealous of you or do they want your job? Do they think you deserved that last promotion? Do they think you're a hard worker?

Family might be the one area we gives ourselves somewhat of a break (but then again, for some it may be an even stronger struggle for approval) but suffice to say, we are seeking approval from *all* the wrong places.
The question remains: why do we care so much about what people think? If we really think about it, it shouldn't matter because:
1) it doesn't change who we are
2) even if you did receive their approval, it's as fickle as the wind. Here one moment, gone the next.

Seeking others' approval doesn't get us any further ahead, in fact it does the opposite-it causes us to backslide. We get bogged down with the emotions of it all because, let's get real here-we will never, ever, ever live up to everyone's expectations. We are human. We make mistakes. We screw things up. And even when we are humble about that, it still disappoints others and ourselves. We aren't meant to be perfect and we never will be. So even with all the striving to be the best baker or the best hairdresser or the best mother-it will never be enough and it will always leave them wanting more. That's why it's important to know who we are in Christ. And He is always excited and ready to tell us. He isn't standing up in heaven, pointing His finger down at us and telling us to "get it together," He is constantly trying to get us to sit down and rest with Him. True rest. True peace. Rest and peace that only come from spending time in the quiet with God. That's Holy rest. And it heals so many wounds, too numerous to count. We may think we're doing God the favour by sitting with Him and being in His presence or practicing His rest but truly, we are doing ourselves the favour. We get to recharge our batteries to head out into the world we live in. It's rough out there! There's so much coming at us from so many different directions. And it's exhausting! Yet, God knows we need that rest. And He desires to give it to us if we stop long enough to receive it.

### *The importance of devotion and spending time with God*

Think about your spouse. Or your child. You have a deep desire to sit down and spend some real quality time with them. Some one-on-one time. You've been waiting all day. The time comes around and your child or spouse is busy, being interrupted by their phone. You try to get their attention again. The next thing you know the dog has run out the back door and you have to go chase after him. You sit back down and they're back on their phone again, saying they 'can hear everything you're saying' and 'not to worry, I'm listening.' Do you feel like they're even present? No. Because they're not giving you their attention. They may be merely feet away yet they're galaxies away in relation to attention. There's no connection there or active listening going on. It is the same as if you were in two different rooms on two different floors.

Sometimes I think God feels that way. We spend time praying with Him but the nano-second that phone buzzes to alert us, we are so incredibly quick to check it, rather than to turn off the distractions and really spend time with God. It's in those times of rest and quiet that God speaks most clearly to us. He's waiting for us to quiet our minds and souls long enough for Him to start speaking to us. And that…my friend…is the sweet sauce. That's when He's able to share His love with you, share how He sees you, who He says you are and who you find yourself to be in Him. That, is a blessed, beautiful gift. Yet so often we are too busy to receive it.

We live in a world that is full of distractions. We also live in a world that's full of addictions, even though we would be offending our 'delicate senses' to call it that. But that's the truth. Back in 'Bible times' that would be called an idol. Even though we don't dip it in gold and actively worship these addictions, they have become idols in our lives. It can be anything that takes away your time with God:

**T.V:** This is a huge problem today. Television is literally around us everywhere. When you go out to eat it's at the restaurant, it's in our homes, its now on fridges and cellphones and everywhere you turn. Now with apps like Netflix, people can 'binge-watch' entire seasons and lock themselves into a whole different world. Hours pass by and with no commercials in-between, there's no awareness of how much time has been spent 'plugged in' to the show.

**Technology:** (cellphones, iPads, iPods). They're everywhere. It seems almost everyone has one now. I have seen anywhere from 3 year-olds to 90 year-olds own one of these devices. Children are exposed at younger and younger ages now and the science that is now coming out about the damaging effects of these devices on little minds and bodies is alarming. Yet, sales are at an all-time high and I don't see the trend going away anytime soon.

**Food:** We can hide behind the label of 'foodie' or lover of food but this is another huge idol in today's society. Just look at the data behind obesity rates in the U.S and even Canada. It has skyrocketed beyond what anyone could have imagined. I, myself, have struggled with the lie at one time or another, that I 'deserve' to treat myself. I am very health conscious and always strive to eat healthy but at times when the temptation is there, sometimes I give in. And that's ok sometimes, in moderation but I'm speaking of the larger issue. The world tells you that you should be treating yourself all the time. Marketing is targeted at selling the 3 human cravings: salt, fat and sugar. People are more concerned with the high they get from eating something delicious to them, then the fact that they should be fuelling their body with nutrients. It's become more about *what feels good* than what is needed.

I know the list is much larger than this but this is to demonstrate just a few. There's also the obsession/addiction to being *young and beautiful*, and so many more. These addictions have become idols in our lives. They become more important that the time spent with God. That is by definition, what an idol is. Yet, we don't often stop and think about that. It's not talked about. It's shoved under the rug.

Between the distractions and addictions all around us, it takes dutiful determination to purpose time with God. The most mind-blowing part of it all is that time spent with God is the only thing that gives us enough of what we need in order to survive this crazy world we live in. Stopping all the noise and distractions, is being researched more and more and the data keeps concluding that we need rest, we need time to get 'unplugged' from it all and we need to slow down as a society. The amount of retreats out there that claim to 'rejuvenate' and 'escape' in order to relax, are solely based around the idea of getting away from technology, busy-ness of life and distractions. And they work...however, the moment you get home you're thrown right back into it all and all the rejuvenation you experienced has just been washed down the drain. Why? Because it can't be based on a one-time experience. You would need to be living in that environment every day in order to reap the benefits of it every day. It is the *same* when it comes to spending time with God. You can't expect to spend one day a month, for an hour, with God and experience the fullness of who He is. Or to get filled up with His truth. Or to rest in His arms of love. You are not made to do life on your own. You are made to do life together, with God. And that comes from spending time with Him. If you leave that to once a month, you won't be experiencing all that you could. Spending time with God is a privilege but how often do we see it as a chore? I know I used to.

I would get determined to spend time with God every day and each day, something would 'come up' that would prevent it. That was before I began to really dive into a deeper relationship with Him. But then I made the decision that I was not going to live in fear anymore and I didn't care what it took. I began studying the Word, reading any books I could on spiritual warfare, and dedicating devotional time with God. I made it my number-one priority and it was interesting how all those former distractions that used to keep 'interrupting me,' no longer were there. I ignored them. I pushed them off and out of my mind. I was determined to spend even 20 mins a day with God. But an interesting thing began to happen. As I stayed committed to spending time with God, my desire grew. I was no longer doing it out of obligation or because I thought I 'had to,' I was doing it because I couldn't wait! And then I went through some tough times in my life where God became my air, and I desperately needed that time with Him everyday or I wasn't going to do well at all. And looking back at what I went though and the huge struggles that were in my life, I can't believe I came through it with such a positive attitude and a huge testimony. Friends and family and those at church who knew some of the struggles I was going through were constantly saying, "I don't' know how you're so positive," or, "I can see your trust in God is helping you get through this," or, "You are a testimony to giving it to God." Now I don't say that to pump my own tires, I say it for the exact opposite-to give God the glory for those times. I couldn't have done it without Him. Truly. He brought me through so many 'valleys of the shadow of death' (Psalm 23), that there were too many to count. But I was only able to go through it because He never left me, and I kept my determination set on spending time with God every day. That's what working together with God is like. He does his part, and you do yours.

Because of those hard times, I grew in faith. I grew in giving God all my trust. I grew in hearing His voice and being more aware of the Holy Spirit and His promptings. I grew in knowing who I am in Christ which led me down the path of finding freedom from fear. I learned so much and that's why I feel so privileged to share it with you. I know God has you on this journey too, and I cannot express enough, the importance of you spending that time with God. It doesn't have to be a fancy devotional or 5 hours a day. It can be simple. It can be reading the Word, journaling your heart to Him, praying or anything that involves spending time with Him. If you can only start with 5 minutes a day, then do it. And I guarantee that the more you do it, the more you'll find time because the more you're want to do it. The more excited you'll be to learn from Him. The more you'll grow in your knowledge and understanding of the Word and His Character. Some days, it will be the air you need to keep going. Other days, it will be the song you whistle all day long. But each day He will be renewing your mind and your heart, and you will see things and believe things you never thought possible. He is amazing that way and He is always faithful.

Journalling was a big part of what worked for me. I always have loved to write but I didn't spend the time journalling. I don't journal about my day though, I journal with God. I think of it as a dialogue with God but also I write down prayers to Him. It's special to be able to look back and see answered prayers so I can give Him thanks. I also write down things I feel God is saying to me and that is probably the coolest thing I have ever experienced in my life-to be able to look back and see the things God has said to me, or prophesied over me that came to pass, or whispered to me to encourage me through the hard times. I believe God used the journal to grow in our dialogue back and forth. It's recorded and it's been a great source of strength to look back and re-read promises or encouragements He's spoken to me. I don't know if you've ever tried journalling before but if not, I encourage you to give it a try. Journal your prayers and verses that God shows you, or be bold and begin to write down what you feel God is saying to you. Don't overthink it-just trust that God will show you the way. If journalling isn't your thing, then find some other ways that speak to you. I also love to worship-playing piano or guitar. Maybe for others that looks like putting on some worship music and just soaking in his presence. Perhaps you like devotional books or bible study's, or just reading through the Word. Whatever it is, make the time to spend with God. Keep that determination strong and don't waver.

You'll be encouraged and that time will be such a blessing to you. If you can make that time to stop, quiet your body and your soul, long enough to listen, you can hear the sweet sound of God speaking truth to you. And one simple truth from God drowns out a thousand lies of the world.

# Chapter 4

## Trust and Faith

As we discovered in the last chapter, entering the rest of God is so integral to alleviating anxiety. Why is that? Rest allows us to shut out all the noises and distractions of the world, and focus on God. It is then that we can receive the truth from God. The truth is that anxiety is based on fears and lies. If you think back to where some of your anxiety started, what lie did you believe in order to lead to the anxiety? I have a simple exercise that is incredibly freeing and allows you to see where the enemy has come in and placed lies. Once you recognize those lies, and that they are in fact lies, they lose their power. They have no hold on you because even if you believe that feeling to be true, you cannot deny that it's a lie. Our feelings are not always honest with us, and when we see that our feelings are based on a lie, it makes it easier to face them and realize the truth.

And really you need to ask yourself one really big question. Ponder this question. Pray about this question. And ultimately dig deep and be really honest: Do you trust God? I won't even ask you to attach a percentage to it because here's the honest truth, either you trust God or you don't. That's it. There's no, "I trust God 80%." You either trust God, or you don't. If your answer is yes, then you will move through this exercise with some amount of ease. If your answer is no, you need to pray about that. Seek God and His reassurance. Repent and ask forgiveness. Ask for the gift of faith. Trust that God will show up, because He always does. Study the Word. Research all the times God was faithful in the Word. All the times He sent His angels to stand guard. His promises about how He takes care of us-it's all throughout the bible! It's quite astounding once you start looking for it. Dwell on those, pray about them, and begin to repair your trust in God.

I would say that trust in God is one of the single-most important things you can do to get on the path to freedom from anxiety. I would say a very close second is faith. When it comes to trust though, I would venture to guess that a huge part of that lack of trust is what lead to your anxiety in the first place. I know that was the case for me. I wasn't trusting that God would take care of me or the situations that came up. I was relying on myself far more than I was relying on God. And it led me to a place of fear because that's a lot of weight to carry on your shoulders. Who can say that they would want the responsibility of their destiny and taking care of all the things in their life that are out of their control? I worried myself sick numerous times because I was worry about things that I couldn't control, even if I wanted to. I would worry and worry and yet, even with all that worry, I would be no further ahead. In fact I would be worse off because on top of the worry, I was making myself sick. It wasn't until I started to really dive into the Word and ask the Holy Spirit to reveal the root of my fear, that I began to understand that at the root of all fear is a lack of trust in God. It was hard to grapple with that because I have been a believer pretty much my entire life, yet, I was struggling with trust in God.

Tied closely to that, is faith. Faith is the things we trust God for and that we hope for:

*"Now faith is the reality of what is hoped for, the proof of what is not seen." Hebrews 11:1 (CSB)*

If we keep our eyes focused on what we don't have and the disappointments we've faced in the past, we are losing the hope that presses us forward in faith. An amazing passage of Scripture to read that really opened my eyes in a transformative way to understating the power of faith is Hebrews 11. Read the entire chapter. It's a description of all the heroes of faith and how we can be assured in our own faith. It is truly a profound chapter in the Bible. It encourages me that if those heroes of faith can believe in such huge and unbelievable things that God asked them to do (like walking into a fiery furnace or building an ark when they land had never even seen rain in years), then I can have faith for the things God has asked of me. I can have faith that I will get stronger in my walk out of fear and worry. I can have faith that good things are going to happen to me. I can have faith that God will do the impossible and that I can have faith in His good plans for me!

When I truly began to trust in God, asking Him to increase my faith (by praying for it!), get self-control over my thoughts and have the Holy Spirit  expose the lies of the enemy, that was when I began to walk in freedom. That was the turning point for me and I believe that will also be the turning point for you. God lifted that burden off of me and put it on His shoulders, where it belongs in the first place. often picture Him (the shepherd) taking me (the lamb) and placing me wrapped around His shoulders as he walks on. And that's really it. That's a picture of what God does for us. He won't do it all for us though, He wants to partner with us. We can pray for anxiety to be miraculously healed and have faith for that (and sometimes God does do a miraculous healing), but often we have a part to play in it, as well. We have some work to do like making the choice to cast our thoughts and making the choice to trust. Thanks be to God, though, that He is so patient with us! And so merciful, generous, gracious and kind to us. He is pastoral in His approach, not abrasive. And He stands there with open arms, ready to receive us in whatever place we are at. But He won't leave us there. That's the beauty of God, He meets us where we are at, but He leads us, hand-in-hand, down the rest of the path.

# Chapter 5

---

## The Next Leg of the Journey

This journey can feel long at times, but it's a blessed one with God leading the way! God isn't ready to leave us in our anxiety or our fear. He wants to deliver us from it, right now! Sometimes He does that through miraculous healing and sometimes He does that through partnership and taking steps with the leading of the Holy Spirit. We have to trust that with each victory over anxiety, God is bringing us to more and more restoration. He is mending your heart and healing areas of your life where the enemy has left scars. Yes, there are scars. They are a reminder but rather than seeing them as a reminder of the hurt, see them as a reminder of the healing! That scar is there because it *did* heal. God didn't leave it bleeding, He mended it and made it stronger. Did you know that scar tissue is stronger than skin tissue? It is! And that serves as an example of God's redemption. We find that to be a truth that's promised in the Word:

*"That is why, for Christ's sake, I delight in weaknesses, in insults, in hardships, in persecutions, in difficulties. For when I am weak, then I am strong." 2 Corinthians 12:10*

*"A cord of three strands is not quickly broken."*
*Ecclesiastes 4:12*


Rather than letting it defeat us, God healed that wound for us and we can be reminded of the healing that took place. Each trial makes us stronger. Sometimes we don't understand why we encounter trials but we do know that:

a)    God can work them for our good! (Romans 8:28)
b)    In this world we will have trials, but He has overcome the world! (John 16:33)
c) God uses the trials to grow us in our faith  (James 1:2-4)


No one wants to go through trials, but yet as believers, one of the gifts we have is that we don't have to go through them alone. Some of my deepest moments of growth and deepest moments of bonding with God, have been in the midst of a storm. My only means of survival are relying on Him and seeing Him work as my strength. There have been moments and seasons in my life where I am hanging on with all I have to the Word and God's voice, and He is my air. When I have nothing left to give, He carries me. I wouldn't want to go through those storms again, but there is no way I would ever want to trade the deepness I grew in, or the closeness of the relationship that I gained, or the beautiful intimacy that came from walking through the storm together. Courage is built in pushing through the storm. Standing still in the middle of the storm not only serves no purpose, but it means you will stay stuck in the storm, you will stay stuck in the pain. When you make the decision to push through with the help of the Holy Spirit, you're pushing past the pain and learning to rely on God to help you take that next step forward. At times it feels slow, and we just want God to make all the 'yuckiness' go away, and He does, but maybe not as quickly as we'd like Him to, or in the way we'd like Him to. But don't discount what is being done in the supernatural, in the unseen realm. God is fighting our battles, when our eyes can't see. When you rely and trust in God to be your victor, and your warrior, you are taking the pressure off of yourself.

Pressure is a terrible motivator. How many times have you felt immense pressure to do something? I know for me that it's a feeling that far-too-often leads me into deep water. I can feel myself being led by my feelings, and the pressure to perform, or get something done, or keep up with something. But we are not called to be led by our feelings, as feelings are fickle. Being led by pressure causes us to begin to let fear set in, and even panic. Once you get to that point, it's hard to turn around. You need to be aware of you motivation before getting to that point. When you are able to be tuned in the Holy Spirit's voice and you notice yourself feeling pressure, that's the moment that you need to stop and assess your motivation. Why are you doing that particular thing? Is it because you're trying to impress someone? Are you feeling overwhelmed and that's why you're putting the pressure on yourself? Is it desperation? Is it boredom? No matter what the motivation behind it is, if any of those motivations lead to feeling pressured, that's the time to stop. Stop and refocus your priorities. Don't let outside influences or stressors cause you to lose your peace. If the task doesn't need to be done immediately, put it aside until you feel that you have the time, energy and emotional dedication that it needs. I promise you, the time WILL come when you can tackle it. And you will enjoy it so much more when you can dedicate yourself to it in those ways. Rushing through it to just hurry and get it done is not only not rewarding, but it causes you to lose your peace and not enjoy the task at hand. Waiting until you are able to dedicate the time and energy to it, will be much more rewarding and peaceful. At the end of the day, peace is the biggest victor against anxiety.

Maybe this isn't an area of struggle for you but for someone like me and I'm sure many others out there, I struggle to stop doing things all the time. I am an extremely determined person, and I'm also very goal-oriented. I also am very ambitious and probably would be described as type A personality. So for someone like me, procrastination isn't a thing...at all. I tend to go the other way which is doing too much and burning myself out. But whatever your personality is, know that pressure shouldn't be a motivator. Peace should always be the motivator for you. If you're feeling overwhelmed or anxious, take a moment to ask yourself what your motivation behind the task is. Ask the Holy Spirit to guide you and bring truth to your understanding.

### *What do you believe?*

As you're moving forward on this next leg of the journey, I want you to remember that you need to make a choice to believe the Word of God, the promises of God, the truth that the Holy Spirit speaks to you, more than anything else. The enemy is going to try and lie to you and put thoughts in your mind that will make you question everything you think, feel and even believe. I know for me, when I really started stepping out in faith, the enemy was even placing thoughts in my mind to make me question my belief in God. It was shocking to me because I had never even once questioned it and I knew the truth in my heart but the enemy was throwing everything he could at me to see what would stick. I had to make a choice: do I believe what I feel or do I believe the Word of God? I knew that I could trust the Bible. I couldn't even always trust what I felt the Holy Spirit was saying at the very beginning because I felt it was based on what I couldn't see, but I did know I could trust the Word of God and that it is truth. I knew that I had to start believing and having faith in the promises of God in the Bible otherwise I would never experience the fullness of what is promised in the Bible. And I so desperately wanted to see those promises come to fruition in my life. So I made the choice to trust the Word, and not my feelings or trust the Word *more* than I trusted my feelings.

### *God's exchange program*

In God's economy, it comes down to an exchange: you keep giving up control and surrender yourself to Him, and God gives you peace in replacement. What a beautiful exchange that is! This was a principle I didn't really understand until recently in my walk with God. It was a revelation that God gave me-the more I give up of myself, my will, my meddling, the more God is able to work in my life and give me the peace to trust in Him to take care of it. It is not a feeling that you have as feelings can be fleeting and fickle, but instead it is a choice that you make to trust God. I spent so many years in self-care (as in taking care of myself), that when God started revealing to me that he wanted to take care of me and for me to let Him, it wasn't an overnight success. I wish it was, but I wasn't ready to give up my will yet. I was stubborn. And then in the moments when I decided that I did want to give it to Him, I felt like I didn't know how. God had to do a work in me to allow me to let go of self and start relying on Him. It took time. Maybe it won't take as long for you, but for me, I had spent so long on self-reliance that the outcome of trust in God took longer than I expected. But just like always, God is faithful and He came through like He always does. He was gentle. It took me taking little baby steps forward each day and He was always gentle with me. He never rushed me but gently encouraged me to keep going. Keep following. Keep seeking. Keep trusting. One step at a time. What a blessing that we have a Father who loves us so much! He is always meeting us where we are not and not pushing but gently encouraging. There is definitely a difference between pushing and encouraging. But God chooses the latter because of His love for us. Be blessed today by God's gentle encouragement to move forward.

Know this truth: GOD WILL NOT LOVE YOU ANY MORE OR ANY LESS IF YOU DON'T TAKE THAT STEP FORWARD. HIS LOVE DOESN'T CHANGE. HE WILL STILL FEEL THE SAME ABOUT YOU. HE WON'T BE MAD AT YOU.

But I would add to that, that you *will* be missing out on the gift He is offering you: to take your hand and walk you through the journey. The beauty of doing it together is that you're not alone and He will be your guide.

*"Fear not, for I am with you; be not dismayed, for I am your God; I will strengthen you, I will help you, I will uphold you with my righteous right hand." Isaiah 41:10*

This is a Bible promise and one that you can declare and proclaim over your life! That's so much better than doing it alone. Take the gift He is offering you today and let Him help you take that first baby step towards freedom.

# Chapter 6

---

## Developing Peace

Peace is such a valuable gift in our lives. To live in peace and harmony is such a seemingly unattainable position. In today's society, the idea of peace is sought after, but rarely attained. Clinics and retreats and wellness centres all over the country claim to give you the rest you need and restore your soul. They promise so many things yet, even if you do find solace and rest, is it still there once you're back home and in the routine of life again? It seems that peace can be stolen in a single instant, and you can go from some amount of peace, to utter chaos or anxiety so quickly. Why is that? And what can be done about keeping peace?

To know how to attain peace, first let's look at what peace is and where it comes from.

The definition from Merriam-Webster dictionary:
***Peace*** is *a state of tranquility or quiet; freedom from disquieting or oppressing thoughts or emotions.*

The Hebrew word for peace is Shalom or šālôm which is defined as *totality or completeness, success, fulfillment, wholeness, harmony, security and well-being.*

True peace can only come from the Author and Perfecter of peace. The One who is Peace personified. The One who doesn't only emulate peace but is in fact, Peace. Trying to attain it in and of ourselves seems logical but it's not possible. God has already given us perfect peace, on the inside of us. How do I know this? It says so right in God's Word.

*"But the Holy Spirit produces this kind of fruit in our lives: love, joy, **peace**, patience, kindness, goodness, faithfulness, gentleness, and self-control." Galatians 5:22-23 (NLT) (emphasis mine).*

*"Peace I leave with you; my peace I give you. I do not give to you as the world gives. Do not let your hearts be troubled and do not be afraid." John 14:27 (NIV)*

And He helps us with these! He guides us along in learning how to walk in them:
*"Surely God is my help; the Lord is the one who sustains me." Psalm 54:4 (NIV).*

I read the verse in John (above) so many times as a believer and never really understood it. If God has already given us peace, and His Word says that it's one of the fruits of the Spirit, and the Spirit lives inside of me, then why do I have anxiety sometimes? Shouldn't it just be available to me when I need it? Here's the truth: it is available to us but you also have to make choices that pursue peace. I've learned for myself that I have to choose it. It means more than choosing to believe in peace. It means choosing trust in God, choosing to trust in His faithfulness. It means choosing to turn off my reasoning and over-thinking and giving those thoughts to God. It means choosing to read His Word and let the truth of the Word cover my heart and soul. It means choosing to believe the best, the positive, that God is taking care of me, despite how I 'feel' inside. God has made our bodies and minds so amazing *and* complex! You can feel something inside but choose to believe something different. I have had many moments where I felt fear of something, but I chose to walk in courage and do it anyways. Because at the end of the day, I want to grow in my faith.

Now when I talk about stepping out and doing something you're afraid of, I am not talking about something that you know to be foolish like walking in front of a car and saying, "I don't want to be afraid of cars anymore so I'll step in front of one and pray that God doesn't allow it to hit me." That would be stupid, I think we can agree. The difference is when you're feeling fear in an area and you know that God doesn't want you to be afraid, that you take the step of faith to trust in God to help you do it. An example of this would be how I used to be afraid of travelling. I was afraid of flying and going away from home and I had so many unfounded fears. I knew that in reality there was an extremely low chance of a plane crash, and that I would be fine if I was away from home, yet my irrational fears always took over. As I began to trust in God more and learn more about the root of my fears, as well as realize the lies the enemy kept telling me, I was able to start taking baby steps towards stepping out in faith. It was definitely hard and it took determination but what I started to realize was that when I did take the little baby steps, I was ok! That was bondage-breaking revelation right there. For example, if I took a day trip with my family a few hours away from home, I was stepping out in faith to do this and I realized that I was ok. That built a little more faith in me for the next time and the next thing. After a while, God gave me the ability to travel abroad with no fear. He was faithful and kept speaking truth to me, I kept resisting the devil's lies and before long, I was walking in freedom in the area of travel. What a blessing to be freed from the fear of travel! It built strength in my marriage (being married to a travel-loving husband!) and with my trust in God. But if I hadn't taken those first baby steps, I wouldn't be walking in freedom today. What I am trying to really impress upon you that is so important is that you will have to be uncomfortable some of the time. God will help you but you have to do the work of stepping out. It won't always feel good and that's when you pray your little heart out and trust God. He will help you through it and He will bless you and lead you down the path to freedom. But stepping out and being uncomfortable in the short term will reap long-term benefits!

I want to grow in trusting God. I want to grow in courage and strength. I know that the only way to do that is to push myself, even if it's only a small step. Staying parked in the middle of the storm doesn't allow me to get out of it any faster, but if I can put one foot in front of the other, I can start to walk out of the storm. And as believers, the most beautiful part is we don't have to walk it alone. God is right there alongside us, giving us the ability if we will ***only*** trust Him.

I compare it to working-out a muscle. The first time you lift a 10 pound weight, it's heavy. Perhaps the first 3 reps are somewhat easy, but after the 4th rep, you begin to feel a little burn in your muscles. You are making micro-tears in your muscle tissue. And those micro-tears are what causes the 'burn' and the pain. If you stop at the moment you feel that it's hard, on that 3rd rep, you will not build those muscles. The next time you pick up that weight and get to the 3rd rep, it will not be any easier than the first time. You could pick up that 10 pound weight each day, for a year, and it will be just as hard on day one, as day 365. It will still feel like a 30 pound weight because you haven't built any muscle. But if, instead, you push past that 3rd rep and go up to 4 or 8 or 10 reps, you begin to build stronger muscle. You won't be able to go from 4 reps to 400 reps overnight, but over time you will build more and more muscle and each time you push yourself past that burn, you will be that much stronger. Before long, you will be increasing the weight you can carry and the stamina of reps.

That is a perfect example of anxiety and how to begin to overcome it. The first time you feel fear, if you try to ignore it, it would be the same as stopping the weight at the 3rd rep. You aren't pushing yourself to face it. You aren't doing anything to push past the fear. You are staying in the middle of it. But if, instead, you take a step, even if it's only one step, you've now grown that 'courage muscle' a little bit. And if each time you feel fear, you push yourself just a little bit further the next time, and the next time, and the next time, before you know it, that big mountainous fear becomes nothing but a wimpy little 10 pound weight, instead of what felt like a 30 pound weight. And the more reps you do, the more times you step out in faith and courage, the more you build those muscles of courage, faith in God, trust in God and stamina in the next battle. It encourages you more and more. Things that were huge barriers and fears in your life before, are now easier to conquer. Issues that felt like mountains before are now only ant-hills. Ant-hills that you can step over and be on your way.

Peace is like that, too. The more you step out in courage, the more it builds peace. Because peace is really trust in God. If you break it down to it's core principal, peace is trust. That may seem backwards that I'm telling if you take a step out into something uncomfortable, that it will produce peace. It won't happen immediately but as you take those steps you will build courage and that courage will lead you to see you can overcome the fears and overcoming fear, leads to peace. Let me give you an example to help explain this point.

## *Trusting from a young age*

Children, generally speaking, at a young age, trust their parents. Now I know there are children who come from abusive homes, or foster care or difficult situations. I am not referring to those kinds of situations in this example. I am speaking to situations in which a child is raised in a loving home. I am not discounting that there are children who aren't raised in loving homes, because I know that absolutely exists and it's sad and tragic, but for the purposes of this example, I am speaking to the loving homes of most children.

Children, generally speaking at a young age, trust their parents. From newborn to toddler and beyond, they trust that their parents will take care of them. They trust that their parents will feed them. They trust that if they get a scrape, they'll nurse the wounds. They believe that their parents want to bring them (their children) joy. Children understand this from a small age. Young children have that ability to trust and in that satisfaction, they are at peace. I have never met a typical toddler who runs around worrying that their mom is not going to feed them. I have never met a toddler who is stressing about their mom and dad's bank account figure. I have never met a toddler who is worrying about if their parents will give them a place to sleep, or if they get a cold or a scrape, whether or not their mom or dad will give them what they need to get better. And because of that, children are generally peaceful. That doesn't mean their are children who don't have anxiety, because there are, but again I'm speaking in general. Most children have a deep-rooted belief that their parents love them and are taking care of them.

How much *more* does our Father in heaven love and take care of us? It's much more immeasurable and surpassing than we can ever even ask or imagine. Let's look at some Scripture with this promise.

*"For I know the plans I have for you," declares the Lord. "Plans to prosper you and not to harm you, plans to give you a hope and a future." Jeremiah 29:11 (NIV).*

*Now to him who is able to do immeasurably more than all we ask or imagine, according to his power that is at work within us," Ephesians 3:20 (NIV).*

At the root of their peace is a trust in their parents. And at the root of our peace, is a trust in our Father. Just read through Psalm 91, about being under the shadow of the Almighty, how He shelters us from storms and protects us. Whether your anxiety is related to finances or fame, health or crowds, animals or being in public…there are thousands of phobias but the point here is that it doesn't matter what the fear is based around because the answer is the same for all of them. ***The solution doesn't change based on the problem.*** The solution is the same for all of them. The solution lies in trust. Trust in God that He is taking care of you. Trust in God that He has your answer and that He's working it out, right now. Right ***now***. He is working on your solution. He is working out your victory. He is working in the unseen realm to bring a victory that is better than we could even ask or imagine. Do you believe that? I know perhaps in your head you could say that but do you believe it in your heart, mind, soul and with all your strength? (see Matthew 22:37).

I know that trust is a question I grappled with for so many years. I didn't even know I was struggling with this question. I hadn't thought about trust, I hadn't pondered it. But one day I heard a sermon in which the preacher said, "Either you trust God…or you don't. There's no percentage tally here. Ask yourself, do you trust God, or don't you?" And I realized that was part of my struggle with anxiety. I had trusted God in many areas of my life, but I still had my hand over here in my health concerns and over here in my financial issues. And I also had my little backup plan over here *just* in case He didn't come through in this or that area. And I trusted Him 85% in this one area, but that other 15% I was unsure of so I controlled the situation for that 15% of the time, just in case-as my backup. As I began to look at different areas of my life, I realized that I wasn't fully putting my trust in God. And part of that was due to the fact that I was afraid. The enemy had spent so much time whispering worries in my ear that I began to believe them. They weren't true, but they were *just* convincing enough that they seemed logical and then they turned into my truth. It was crazy to look back and see how many lies I believed because I didn't take the time to pray about a situation and instead I just believed whatever popped into my head.

One situation that comes to mind is around the area of relationships. Early on in my life, I had a friend who made it her mission in life, to find out who was important to me and try to break up our friendship. If she knew I liked a certain boy, she'd get it out of me who it was, and then exploit that information and seek to get this boy to like or date her instead, in order to hurt me. Or if I had a close friend, and she felt that my friend and I were happy or growing closer, she would tell that friend terrible lies about me in an attempt to 'steal' their friendship and alienate me from my close friend. I now know it was because of her own insecurity but at the time, it was **extremely** painful and

I didn't understand it. I didn't even recognize what a pivotal point that was in my life and how much it affected my adult relationships until a few months ago, during one of my 'Holy Spirit Counselling sessions' as I like to call them, when the Holy Spirit revealed the root of rejection in my life. But God's timing is perfect and I believe He knew I wasn't ready to handle or deal with that reality until recently.

I tell you that story because sometimes the pain we carry today, has a root from the past. And what happens (just like what happened to me), is the enemy took a very painful situation and started feeding lies to me. And without the discernment to pray about it or seek healing or answers to it, I just took the lies at face value and believed them to be true. He often whispers rejecting lies like,
"You're not good enough for _____."
"_____ doesn't like you because you've got __ and ___ problem."
"He'll just get rid of you once he finds someone better."
"You're too bossy for him/her, so they don't like you."
"You're too emotional for him/her so they don't want you."
"It's no wonder they rejected you, you're hard to love."

I mean lie, after lie, after lie was being fed to me and it was subtle enough, and I was young and naive enough to believe it. I was a teenager who had a hundred different emotions and it happened during a very formative time in my life, and my guard was down. So I began to believe them. And I didn't know I was believing a lie, because it felt real. It wasn't until I learned that the enemy speaks lies to us that I really began to question some deep rooted hurts in myself. And I believe the same for you. That you've had some hurts in your past that you have carried through to today. The enemy has used those hurts to make you believe his lies. He exploited you and used those hurts to cause you more pain and make you believe the lies he was feeding you. Most fears stem from a painful experience. And when we are young or impressionable or lack knowledge about the ways the enemy comes against us, it allows those lies to become rooted and we begin to believe them as truths. It's only when we ask the Holy Spirit to come in and reveal the truth about *who* we are and *who we are* in Christ, that we can start to expose the lies, expose the enemy and truly get *free* from the pain of our past. God can open our eyes to the false fears that have been keeping us trapped in our pain, and move forward in the freedom that God offers! Sometimes it's painful to open that door but if we don't, we stay trapped in a prison of fears. And the truth is that so many of the fears we have are based on lies anyways. Once we can have our eyes opened to the lies, we can begin letting the truth in, and stepping out, baby-steps at a time in faith, and that is when God begins stripping away fear and *peace* begins to overtake the fear. It is then that we can see with open eyes, the beauty of the truth. That God is taking care of us. That we can trust and put our hope in Him.

As I just mentioned, sometimes being exposed to those truths are hard. When the Holy Spirit revealed the truth to me during some journal/prayer time, as He began pouring out the truth, I began to cry. Tears streamed out of me in a steady flow as I cried, I journaled and wrote down what God was showing me. It was *so* powerful. It was overwhelming but in a good way. And although it was hard to face the truth of what had happened, somehow, simultaneously, it was the most freeing experience of my life. I didn't feel trapped in a prison of fear or a lack of understanding of why I was always afraid and living in fear of rejection, but instead as God revealed the truth, and it set me free. The tears were free-flowing but they were tears of release and joy that finally I was able to heal from these wounds of past, pray about it and put that pain behind me. I was finally able to walk in forgiveness toward this person who had hurt me, and in that I found so much freedom!

But God doesn't do anything before we are ready. His timing is perfect and He knows when we are ready to face it. He won't push you or reveal things to you that you aren't yet ready to handle.

*"There is a time for everything, and a season for every activity under the heavens." Ecclesiastes 3:1 (NIV),*

So take that beautiful promise and use that as your cue. If God is revealing something painful from your past, to you, or exposing a lie or revealing the truth, that's your cue that it's time. It's your cue that you *are* ready to deal with it. God is ready to take you through the steps of healing and restoration. You *can* do it because He waited until you were ready. That means you have all the emotions and skills and ability and open heart to receive what He's offering you. You are stronger than you think. He knows now is the time and there's a grace He gives you when you're in that place. He gives us grace to deal with the things that He reveals, for that specific time. Don't waste that time that He's given you. It's precious and it's ripe for the harvest. Embrace it and see that inside of that powerful truth is a gift that's waiting to be unwrapped. And that gift is called freedom.

# Chapter 7

## Freedom from Yesterday
## and
## Hope for Tomorrow

It seems that everything these days promises freedom. Freedom from debt: but really it's an agency that just buys your debt. Freedom from pain with medications that inflict new pains or issues. Freedom from life with a fancy vacation. *Escapism* is the new brand of 'freedom' yet it is a false promise. True freedom comes from exposing the lies and revealing the truth. Escaping the truth and just distracting yourself isn't freedom at all.

Think about your body for example. When you go to the doctor because you have a toothache, the root of the issue could be your sinuses or clenching from stress or many other factors. Your tooth is the part that is aching but something else could be causing that ache. That's just where it manifests.

Much like your body, our minds operate in the same way. We feel pain in the area of rejection or loss, and rather than getting to the root of it, we try to just manage the pain.

If the area of pain is rejection, we try to protect ourselves from being put in a position of vulnerability so we cannot get rejected. If the area of pain is loss, we try to close off our hearts to deep relationship because we think we will protect ourselves from feeling loss again if we don't open our hearts up to love. This is what the world tells you, or more-so, the lies the enemy tells you to keep you cycling in your pain. He doesn't want you to find out the root cause of your pain. He would rather you believe the lie that doing anything else but exposing the truth is the answer. He is manipulative and tricky, trying to use our emotions to keep us trapped in the pain. He will give you reasons why you should keep your heart closed off, or whisper doubts in your ear about opening up to a trusted friend. He would rather you live in complete alienation and escapism of your feelings, than to deal with them. If he can keep you trapped in the prison of your cyclical emotions, then He knows you won't be free. If, however, you instead allow the Holy Spirit to come in and pray and ask Him to reveal the truth, I promise you He will. I can't promise that it will happen immediately, but I can promise you that if your heart is seeking, (Matthew 7:7) God will reveal it to you when you're ready to deal with it and the favour that rests upon you will be the courage and the victory you need to overcome it. He says in His Word:

*"Ask and it will be given to you; seek and you will find; knock and the door will be opened to you. For everyone who asks receives; the one who seeks finds; and to the one who knocks, the door will be opened." Matthew 7:7-8 (NIV).*

*"Very truly I tell you, whoever believes in me will do the works I have been doing, and they will do even greater things than these, because I am going to the Father. And*

*will do whatever you ask in my name, so that the Father may be glorified in the Son. You may ask me for anything in my name, and I will do it." John 14:12-14 (NIV).*

Staying trapped in the past hurts us and keeps us in bondage and fear. Fear comes often from either a painful experience in the past or the unknown future. We have to remember that God is the Alpha and the Omega. He's the first and the last. The past and the future (as well as the present). There is not a situation too great that He cannot fix. Fear keeps us trapped in the lie that we cannot be free from our past. Fear keeps us trapped in the lie that we cannot expect good things for fear of disappointment. Those are direct lies of the enemy. And how do I know that? Because he spoke those exact lies to me. He told me that if I would trust in God completely, I would be leaving myself open to being disappointed. He whispered that lie to me enough and it eventually began to become my truth, even though Scripture speaks in direct opposition to that. That is one way you know it's the enemy lies and tricks at work, when it goes directly against Scripture, or even if he tries to twist the truth of the Word. He is often sneaky with 'half-truth's which are still lies. He may sneakily say, "You can trust in God for the small stuff but when it comes to ____ (fill in any fear you have, here), you really should be in control of that. You don't want to be disappointed." He's masterful at trying to convince us that God is not in control.

Often he will come at us with lies when we are weak-either tired or stressed, or during a stressful time like a job loss or the death of a loved one. When our defences are down, he sneaks in and deposits lies. Maybe under normal circumstances we would be aware of his lie, but because our defences are down, that lie sticks a little easier than it normally would. That's why the Word says we are to:

*"Be alert and of sober mind. Your enemy the devil prowls around like a roaring lion looking for someone to devour.Resist him, standing firm in the faith, because you know that the family of believers throughout the world is undergoing the same kind of sufferings." 1 Peter 5:8-9 (NIV).*

Peter warns us of this, that the devil is ready to pounce and deposit lies.

I know from my own struggle with anxiety, that hearing how much the enemy wants to 'get us,' was at times, anxiety provoking for me. I was always waiting for the nex 'attack' from him. I was fearful that he had me in his cross-hairs, ready to aim and fire. I began to focus more on the enemy than I did on my Saviour. It *is* important to know your opponent. And often there isn't enough teaching out there about the enemy. But on the flip side of that, *only* focusing on the enemy and his schemes, takes your eyes of of God and His victorious power. Remember, the devil is not the opposite of God. God has **power, dominion and authority** over the enemy. He is still the ruler of all and the devil has to bow in submission to God:

*"...that at the name of Jesus every knee should bow, in heaven and on earth and under the earth, and every tongu acknowledge that Jesus Christ is Lord, to the glory of Go the Father." Philippians 2:10-11 (NIV).*

Learn about your opponent so that you're watchful and aware of his tricks (as tricky as he is, he often uses the same tricks so you can learn what to be aware of such as guilt and shame), but don't let that cause you to take your eyes off Jesus, the Saviour of the world, your Saviour. Jesus wants us to run to Him and let Him fight our battles for us (see 2 Chronicles 20:15, below), rather than us try to fight our battles on our own. We weren't created to fight with flesh and blood or fight powers and principalities (see

Ephesians 6:12, below).  God wants us to run to Him, to call upon His name and He will be there to fight for us. (see Psalm 9).

*"He said: "Listen, King Jehoshaphat and all who live in Judah and Jerusalem! This is what the LORD says to you: 'Do not be afraid or discouraged because of this vast army. For the battle is not yours, but God's." 2 Chronicles 20:15 NIV)*

*"For our struggle is not against flesh and blood, but against the rulers, against the authorities, against the powers of this dark world and against the spiritual forces of evil in the heavenly realms." Ephesians 6:12 (NIV)*

Rather than live in fear of the enemy, arm yourself with:
- Scripture
- the armour of God (Ephesians 6:10-18)
- prayer
- speaking the Word back to the enemy like Jesus did (Matthew 4:1-11)

Just as a good earthy father would fight to protect His child from an enemy, so does our Heavenly Father, but even much more. Because His love is perfect. And as we read in 1 John 4:18, *"There is no fear in love. But perfect love drives out fear, because fear has to do with punishment."* The one who fears is not made perfect in love but instead, perfect love casts out fear. So if we translate **perfect love** to **God**, God casts out fear. And there is power in the name of Jesus. Call upon God to be your Vindicator and speak the name of Jesus. At the name of Jesus every knee shall bow!

On top of that, we have been given the authority in heaven and on earth (Luke 10:19) because of Jesus and His sacrifice. God has given us the ability to have authority over the enemy. God will still fight our battles for us, and work on our behalf, but I believe we have a job as well. To stand firm in faith, like we read in 1 Timothy 6:12: "*Fight the good fight of the faith.*" Co-labouring with our Lord (1 Corinthians 3:9) means that God may give us a part to do. Sometimes that's as simple as making a stand, or a decision in your heart to not give into fear. Or taking a stand to trust God. When I say, 'sometimes that's as simple as', I did not say 'easy.' I was careful with my word choice there because simple and easy are different. In this case, it's not complicated to make a choice to trust God. One would say that's simple, based on ability. But easy would imply that it isn't hard to do. And that's where I want to be clear that although it's simple, it can be hard. It's not easy to look fear in the face and not feel fear. It's not easy to keep choosing to step out in courage when you feel fear but I promise you that the reward is great. And on top of that, God is right there beside you, transforming your mind (Romans 12:2) and doing a work inside of you to change your heart from fear to trust. I don't know how He does it, but I do know that He does. I myself, am proof that God can take someone who lived in fear, and day by day, change them to start trusting in Him and leave fear behind. It takes choice. And persistence. And perseverance. And determination. And a making up of your mind that you will continue to trust in God, no matter what thoughts come into your mind to make you doubt that choice. You *can* do this, and God is reaching out His hand, and asking you to take that first step. The first step is sometimes the hardest, but with each step you take, it *does* get easier and easier, the longer you persevere. And if ever you feel that fear is rising in your mind, speak the truth out loud: either some Scripture verses that are important to you in this area or speaking the truth of who you are in Christ.

Below are two examples I speak out loud. One is of some scriptures that I speak, that I feel have profound impact in the area of trust and of letting go of fear. These are one that I find particularly useful but I encourage you to pray about it and see which scriptures God reveals to you. If you don't have any at the moment, please be encouraged to use these. And remember, to write them down and memorize them if you can, and speak them out loud. When you're speaking the Scripture back to the enemy, it is a form of warfare. Look these up and print or write them out.

- 2 Timothy 1:7
- 1 John 5:14
- 1 John 2:27
- Isaiah 41:10
- 2 Corinthians 5:21
- Isaiah 54:17
- Deuteronomy 28:7
- Romans 8:1
- Philippians 1:6
- Philippians 4:6-7
  *there are so many more but add to this list. Another resource is to search on a search engine, "who I am in Christ" list of verses!

The second thing that I do, is pray truth over myself, about who I am in Christ. I speak it out loud and I cannot emphasize enough, how important it is to speak these words out loud. It changes and shifts the atmosphere. Remember, there is an entire spiritual realm that we do not see, and sometimes that involves speaking things out that need to be said. As we read in Matthew 4:1-11, the devil spoke to Jesus and Jesus spoke back to the devil with Scripture. That was how He defeated the devil and caused him to flee. We have that same authority that's been given to us through Jesus, and it's in our ability to use it, so do it!

Again, with these words that I pray below, you are welcome to use and speak this as well. I believe there is power in speaking these words and they've been great weapons for me. But, I encourage you to pray from the heart and see if there's anything God is putting on your heart to pray. It's not so much about the words as it is about the heart. It doesn't have to be long. It doesn't have to eloquent. Speak and pray from a place of trusting God and the rest will fall into place.

### *I will pray something like this:*

"I speak the name of Jesus over me, right now. I pray the power of the blood of Jesus over my body, my home and my family. I am bought by the blood of Jesus and He is my Saviour. I am a child of God. I am the righteousness of God in Christ. I am the head and not the tail. I am under the wing of the Almighty and He is my Provider, Protector, and Vindicator. No weapon formed against me shall prosper. I will fear no evil for God is with me. He is my rock and my salvation. He is my shepherd. He is my light. I rebuke you Satan in the name of Jesus. You must flee before me in the name of Jesus.I am a child of God. Goodness and mercy will follow me all the days of my life. His plans for me are good!"

It's usually something like that. And it may be a little different each time but that's an outline of what I pray. And I know that it changes atmospheres because I have seen the noticeable change in my attitude, mindset, emotions and feelings after I declare that truth out loud. I have also noticed it encourages me to believe it through and through, and deep in my soul, when I continue to say these truths out loud.

Something that I firmly believe in is this: the Bible is th

Word of God. It is alive (Hebrews 4:12). It is truth. And if I can find it in the Word of God, then I can believe it and trust it. So when I pray, or when I declare things out loud, I pull things from Scripture to guide me. Because if it's Scriptural, then I can stand on it. I can trust it is true and a promise of God. If you do create your own declarations, be sure that they are based in the Word of God.

# Chapter 8

---

## Who Are You Feeding?

I once heard a tale about a man with two wolves. It goes like this:

*An old Cherokee is teaching His grandson about life:*
*"A fight is going on inside me," He said to the boy.*

*"It is a terrible fight and it is between two wolves. One is evil–He is anger, envy, sorrow, regret, greed, arrogance, self-pity, guilt, resentment, inferiority, lies, false pride, superiority, and ego."*

*He continued, "The other is good – He is joy, peace, love, hope, serenity, humility, kindness, benevolence, empathy, generosity, truth, compassion, and faith. The same fight is going on inside you–and inside every other person, too."*
*The grandson thought about it for a minute and then asked His grandfather: "Which wolf will win?"*
*The old Cherokee simply replied, "The one you feed."*

This tale really impacted me on many levels and I think of it often. It's so evident that we have choices about how we think. We can be negative or positive. Kind or mean. Gentle with ourselves or harsh with ourselves. A perfect book that really describes this internal battle going on in the mind is my all-time favourite book, *Battlefield of the Mind* by Joyce Meyer. This is the book that I read that changed my mind and changed my life actually, as far as winning the battle over negativity and fear. As I've shared earlier, I lived in a constant state of fear. I was afraid of decisions, and work and every aspect of my life. I didn't realize that I could actually think about what I'm thinking about, and change my mindset. Joyce's book is a NY Times bestseller for a reason, because it's helped set hundreds of thousands, even millions of people free from fear. We have to start talking about these things and addressing them, but not from the ***world's*** perspective, from the ***Word's*** perspective. *Battlefield of the Mind,* taught me so much about taking control of those thoughts with the guidance of the Holy Spirit and really learning to start thinking in a positive way and not letting the enemy get a foothold in my mind. The battle is in the mind and if we can win the battle in our mind with the Holy Spirit's help, we have won the battle in all the other areas too.

Paul wrote, "I have learned the secret to being content." (Philippians 4:11). He goes on to say that it has nothing to do with life's circumstance, but everything to do with his mindset. And that's so true. If we wait for our circumstances to be favourable, and that is what determines our attitude and joy, then we will be waiting our entire lives to be happy because circumstances aren't always favourable, in fact there is typically a lot of things going on in life that aren't ideal. Bills, health struggles, work stress, life stress-all these things are going on in varying levels each day or week. And if we allow those to dictate our emotions, we are giving away the winning hand. I cannot say that I 'have learned the secret to being content' 100% of the time, but I can say with absolute certainty that I am winning that battle more and more each day, and taking back more and more ground because I put my hope and trust in God that He is going to show me the way. And He does! And I am so grateful for that.

Back to the tale and it's connection to this discussion. In the tale, the grandfather is correct in saying that there's a battle going on in all of us. That battle is really good vs evil. We know that God is good and He lives on the inside of us. And the enemy, the devil, is evil and he is constantly trying to trip us up, hurt us and bring us down in any and all ways that he can.

*"The thief comes only to steal and kill and destroy; I have come that they may have life, and have it to the full." John 10:10 (NIV).*

A lot of the battle is spiritual, but there is some that is also fleshly (meaning of our choices/mentally). See, we co-labour with God (1 Corinthians 3:9) and that means that God has a part that He does (that we cannot do) and we have a part to do that works in harmony with what God is doing. It's an amazing gift that God gives us, to work ***on*** us, ***in*** us and ***through*** us, but we also have a part. And when it comes to 'feeding the wolf' we want to choose the right one to feed. If we want courage and faith, trust and hope, we will want to feed the good wolf. That means choosing to think and meditate on positive things, and choosing to meditate on the Word of God. It also means putting into your mind what you want you come out. In fact, in Scripture, we are instructed to do exactly this (see Philippians 4:8). Paul knew the power of keeping our mind fixed on these things. And now, thousands of years later, research has caught up with what God had instructed us, all along. When you continue to focus on the negative things: past hurts, un-forgiveness, scary situations that happened to you, you are in fact breeding more anxiety and fear. You are feeding the 'evil' wolf and that is what is going to win.

Choosing to think positively, meditating on the truth and Scripture sounds like the right choice and I'm sure everyone wants to do that, but I want to be fair in telling you that it does take work. You have to be committed to choosing it-and choosing it moment by moment, second by second sometimes-especially at the beginning. Our brains are actually creating pathways each day, and I will talk more about this later, but neuroplasticity is new ground-breaking research that speaks about how you can create new pathways in your brain. Without going into too much detail, when you are thinking negatively or drawing your attention back to past experiences, you are actually reliving those feelings and emotions exactly the same as when you actually lived that moment in the past. Your brain has a pathway built into that painful experience and the more you think about it, the bigger that pathway becomes. And the more and more and more you dwell on it, it actually turns into what is called a 'highway in your brain'. Now, that memory and those feelings and emotions come to your mind more easily and are less easily forgotten or pushed away. The more you feed it, the bigger it gets.

But I have amazing news! God doesn't leave us in our mess, He's the Creator and He's created a way out for you! Neuroplasticity is the ability for your brain to be formable, meaning you can actually shut down those negative highways and create new positive highways! And it's not complicated at all, but like I said earlier, it will take some work and dedication. I will get more into neuroplasticity more in the next chapter but I just wanted to give a brief idea of the good news coming to give you hope that you can do this!

Back to positive thinking. It's going to take work. Those negative pathways have created a pattern in your brain and your mind and so when you're tired, or bored, or not paying attention, your mind will naturally revert back to thinking about your most common thoughts. For me, it was fear-related things. For example, if I heard my kids coughing, I would instantly remember a terrible sickness one of them had and I would immediately begin to fear that this was going to repeat itself. It could be a completely harmless cough, yet my brain was programmed to think back to that worrisome experience and I would begin to fixate my thoughts on that. Or another time it would be a friend saying something that made me feel hurt, and I would remember back to when I was deeply hurt by a friend in the past, those same emotions were felt. I would not even notice that I was thinking about it and then minutes later I'd be upset and have no idea why! I would find myself being short-tempered with my family or wanting to be alone and had no idea why-well it was because I was filling my mind with these negative emotions, feelings and memories and even though those experiences were in the past, by thinking about them and dwelling on them, I was reliving all those same painful emotions all over again. And it would happen so quickly, without warning.

It took time to first:
- recognize what I was thinking about
- realize I was dwelling on that negative feeling/memory
- stop thinking about it and pray immediately (out loud if possible)
- refocus my mind to the positive

…but I did get there and I did start to be able to make those changes.

It took time. At first, I wouldn't realize when I was heading down that 'negative thinking highway' but after much prayer asking God to show me and reveal when I was, and being attentive to my thoughts, I started to recognize it. I want to encourage you that you *can* do this. If I can do it, you can do it, too. If God can do it for me, He can do it for you. The beauty of being a follower of Christ is that we aren't doing this alone. God is here to help you and He promises that He will. The proof is in His Word and in the experiences of so many! Look at all the times He promises this:

*"Ask and it will be given to you; seek and you will find; knock and the door will be opened to you." Matthew 7:7 (NIV).*

*"Take delight in the LORD, and he will give you the desires of your heart." Psalm 37:4 (NIV).*

*"In my distress I called to the LORD; I cried to my God for help. From his temple he heard my voice; my cry came before him, into his ears." Psalm 18:6 (NIV).*

*"Yet the LORD longs to be gracious to you; therefore he will rise up to show you compassion. For the LORD is a God of justice. Blessed are all who wait for him!" Isaiah 30:18 (NIV).*

*"May the God of hope fill you with all joy and peace as you trust in him, so that you may overflow with hope by the power of the Holy Spirit." Romans 15:13 (NIV).*

*"Have I not commanded you? Be strong and courageous. Do not be afraid; do not be discouraged, for the LORD your God will be with you wherever you go." Joshua 1:9 (NIV).*

*"No temptation has overtaken you except what is common to mankind. And God is faithful; he will not let you be tempted beyond what you can bear. But when you are tempted, he will also provide a way out so that you can endure it." 1 Corinthians 10:13 (NIV).*

Verse after verse after verse of his continual promises! I could quote at least 50 scriptures where God promises to walk you through this, but I think it's important you for *you* to take the time to look and find some. Use a search engine online or the bible app or whatever source you want to, but I really think its important to start to rely on God to show you what verses He wants to share with you. Finding a verse that God leads you to is much more rewarding and personal than being given the verses. It's still useful and purposeful, but I encourage you to take the time in prayer and in the Word because that's where God speaks to us and we learn the intimacy of knowing Him and seeing what He wants to say to you personally about trusting in Him.

He wants to take you on this journey of intimacy with Him. He wants you to learn the tools but not to rely on yourself to do it, even if the only thing you can say is, "God, show me the way out." I pray this Scripture often (1 Corinthians 10:13, see above) because sometimes I don't even know the answer or the way. I just know I can't do it alone and I need God's help. And each and every time, He has led me the right way. (see Proverbs 16:9). I want to be very clear: *you have a job to do but you cannot do it in your own strength*. You need to rely on God to help you, guide you and transform your mind. Ask him continually.

Pray throughout the day. If you try to just do it by your own willpower, you will end up frustrated. Give it to God and let him lead and guide you to freedom!

For example, I was having a health issue where I would get this tingling sensation in my legs and it was quite concerning to me. I was searching online answers and my doctor wasn't quite sure what it was, and I was going through a season where I felt God was wanting me to rely on Him completely. Not on anyone else, especially not myself. My personality is that I'm a determined person who won't give up, but sometimes to my own detriment. I will push and push to find answers but not stop to listen to the Lord's still, small voice. So during this season, I was really feeling God impressing upon my heart to just trust in Him for the answer. Boy, was I annoyed to wait on Him when I wanted the solution immediately. Here I was, feeling this icky feeling in my legs and God wants me to wait on Him? But I did. I made a promise to myself that I wasn't going to search answers online anymore. And I wasn't going to worry. And I asked the Holy Spirit to help me, fully aware I was weak in my own flesh to do so. I said out loud, "God I trust you to take care of me. And I ask you to show me the way out." I prayed that for a few days and then one day I was on my bed, doing my devotions and God just dropped into my heart, the word 'magnesium.' And I was like, "What?" And I felt God say again, 'magnesium.' I thought, "Well this is quite strange. Magnesium?" But then I remembered my prayer to God and I thought "Well maybe this is the answer."

That afternoon I went to the store and I picked up some magnesium. I cannot tell you the joy that overcame me, when that terrible tingle in my legs left me only a few hours after I started taking the magnesium. I was elated! And I was so grateful to God that He showed me the way. I now take it daily and the feeling has never returned. And it was actually the first of many miracles that God performed in my body. He was waiting for me to let go of myself, and my ambition, my worry (that was a *huge* part of what He was trying to deliver me from) and my stubborn personality that I have to take care of myself. I retired from self-care. God is our physician! God is our healer! God is the one who takes care of us! He knows our entire being, the number of hairs on our head, the way we were knit together. Modern medicine has so many benefits and yes, it can definitely be used by God but we have taken that to be end-all in our society and as believers, it's backwards. We should be going to God first and letting Him direct our steps. He knows us so intimately and He can so quickly fix whatever is wrong because He's the one who knows what's wrong without doing any blood tests or exams. It has been such a lesson in trusting Him to take care of me and to let go of my own determination to take care of myself.

### *Triggers*

When I speak about anxiety, we all have those triggers and those things that really get us going down the path of fear or worry. I still have to take my thoughts captive each day and I notice that when I don't, I can feel it. I've come such a long way in not letting fear have a hold on me by trusting in God. That's why I was so led to write this book, to try to share what God has taught me to be able to hopefully set someone else free! To share the words that God has spoken over me, to share the Scripture He's put on my heart that has helped heal my heart, to share my story to let you know that you're not alone and that someone else is walking alongside you. That's what builds each other up-knowing you're not in it alone and that someone else has walked this road, and come out on the other side. I know that you can do this because I did it. And I was a mess of fear and worry But God has freed me ways I never thought possible.

I also want to be realistic and tell you that I don't ever get full of myself that I'll never have fear visit me again. That's unrealistic. There will be times when fear will try to get to me, but I now have the tools that God's given me to be aware and fight the battle in the mind. But even more than that, I put my trust in God that I am letting Him take care of me. I am giving the battle to God, and letting Him fight for me because that's what He says He will do. (2 Chronicles 20:15). I know that He will fight for me, because He always, always, always has, and He is FAITHFUL! And His faithfulness doesn't run out-He is the same yesterday, today and forever. And that's a promise we can hold onto and enjoy! That is the hope that He offers to us and because of that, I can hope on in faith. I can trust Him. If fear does try to show it's face again, I have the ability to stand firm on all the promises of God and watch Him fight that battle. That right there, is freedom. Freedom to let go of the past and give those thoughts to God. Allowing Him to transform my mind. That is a *daily* prayer of mine. And its so important. Because I need it! And He does change my mind and my heart daily. He increases my faith. He builds me up. He changes my mindsets. He allows me to forget the past and press forward. He allows me to forgive and let go. He allows me to give it to Him. All those things are freedom!

### *Gratitude*

We have a choice to make: *negativity,* which leads to fear or *positivity,* which leads to peace. Just like the tale of the two wolves, whichever one we feed is the one that wins and one of the qualities that breeds peace and freedom, joy and hope…is gratitude. Being grateful for the things you have. Being present and recognizing the things around you that you can be grateful for. *The small things that we take for granted each day can be meaningless if we don't take the time to appreciate them.* The big things that we forget to stop and be grateful for can start to feel owed to us if we aren't careful. Taking time to appreciate those things in the moment is so important. At times when I was feeling anxious, I would stop and just appreciate what I had around me. It did two things:

1) it took my mind off of my worry/anxiety
2) it switched my mindset from worry to gratitude. It created a new pathway in my brain that was geared toward positivity rather than negativity.

It took practice. And time. And choosing it. But more than all that, I know the Holy Spirit was working through me. My prayer was constantly, "God, show me the way out. Help me do this. I know I can't do it alone." And He was faithful, oh so faithful. Practicing being grateful, appreciative, thankful and aware of the blessings around you changes your mindset. Rather than creating pathways that are negative and lead down the path of anxiety and fear, worry and dread, instead create pathways of joy and courage, gratefulness and peace which when practiced, turn those pathways into highways. Which wolf will you feed?

# Chapter 9

---

## Neuroplasticity

This is a topic that I *love*. Yet, I am not a 'sciency' person (Yes, I know that's not a word but doesn't it so perfectly describe it?). In fact, the only part I liked about science class in school, was the experiments. If I was able to take the abstract knowledge I had learned and was then able to apply it to something practical, real, measurable and visually see, then I was excited! I loved dropping eggs from higher floors or seeing a balloon explode off the top of a pop bottle. I am driven towards seeing knowledge applied and watching the things I've learned, turn into something useful.

That's why I'm really excited to share about neuroplasticity.

Why?

Because this topic is going to build hope inside of you. It is going to plant the seeds of hope, even if it's only as small as a mustard seed, inside of you. With practice and the leadership of the Holy Spirit, you'll be watering the seed. And then with persistence, you'll be seeing the first little stem poke its head out of the ground. And with determination, you'll see that elegant stem twist it's way out the soft soil and stretch it's long, muscular back towards the gleaming sun, stretching and moving its way upward to the sky. And before long, that once-tiny seed will be a grand plant that begins to bear fresh, juicy fruit. That fruit will start off slow but as the plant matures, soon there will be a bountiful harvest, baskets overflowing with ripe fruit for the picking. Does this excite you? I hope so because hope is the cornerstone of what will help guide you through this journey of stepping out of anxiety and into courage, freedom and the powerful life God has waiting for you. And a puzzle piece that helps connect us on the next step of our pathway, is neuroplasticity.

Neuroplasticity is: *The brain's ability to reorganize itself by forming new neural connections throughout life.*

Neuroplasticity allows the neurons (nerve cells) in the brain to compensate for injury and disease and to adjust their activities in response to new situations or to changes in their environment (medicine net).

In plain terms, neuroplasticity is the brain's ability to heal itself and when introduced to new environments, thoughts or situations, adapt and create new neutrons which create new pathways in the brain. Much research has been done on the connection between neuroplasticity and anxiety, and there are several books on this topic. I haven't read any of them before learning this concept, but instead it was God that led me to this connection, so I was excited to see that there was also research out there confirming this connection.

In an article written by Thrive Global, they list the benefits of neuroplasticity in the brain, when pertaining to anxiety. Based on their research, you can:

- Delete brain connections between fear and triggers
- Change your habits
- Reduce stress to improve mental health
- Ability to reconstruct your brain to be less anxious
- Change the way your brain reacts to certain situations
- Increase positivity and optimism
- Reduce/eliminate negativity and pessimism
- Alleviate symptoms of anxiety
- Eliminate anxiety
- Change the way anxiety affects you

When looking at that list, neuroplasticity sounds amazing. It sounds like science has found the cure-all but we forget one small thing: we serve a God who created all of it! He is bigger than all of it! And He has given us the ability to have things like scientific evidence, but we must not let that take away the power of our faith to believe that God can do anything. The glory belongs to God. He is the author of neuroplasticity. He created our amazing brains and our ability to adapt and create new pathways. He led scientists to study this and experiment with it and publish studies and books on it. He is in and through it all and I just want to point out that in this journey, you can be grateful for what science has been able to prove, but always be ever-aware that God is the one who created it. Give Him the glory and the praise, give Him the credit for the journey you're on. Remember, He led you here! As you walk this out, also know that He gives you the ability to change. He is working on you right now, and continues to work on you each day, every moment. Your brain is highly complex but it is also highly adaptable. That's why we've been able to adjust and adapt to new environments in jobs, relationships and situations. We have the ability to do it, and we must be willing to put the work in, in order to see the results.

There's an amazing book called, *A Stroke of Insight: A Brain Scientist's Personal Journey*, and it is an autobiography of a neuroscientist who experienced a stroke, and she knew exactly what was happening to her because of her scientific knowledge. She in fact survived the stroke and then began the journey of rewiring her brain. It was because of neuoplasticity that she was able to accomplish this. If you're interested in learning more about neuroplasticity, I encourage you to read it.

For the sake of time and the purpose of this book, I won't dive much into the details about neuroplasticity, but I wanted you to be aware of it, and understand a little of the science behind it because it is an exciting discovery that really encourages us, and brings hope to us that we can do the work and reap the rewards of rewiring our brain. It's a tool that you can learn about and use in this journey. Neuroplasticity is:

- the practice of retraining your mind to focus on the positive
- the practice of creating new habits through repetition
- evaluating your beliefs and determining in your mind to change the negative ones and keep your mind focused on the positive ones
- visualizing your goals and dreams, devoting time to sitting and picturing it. Include your emotions and feelings in this.

All of these steps can be practiced daily, 10-15 minutes each. The research behind it is amazing. Take some time to do some research about neuroplasticity and the steps you can take daily to retrain your brain.

I believe that 80% of our attitudes, feelings, emotions and outcomes are controlled by the brain and if we let our mind run wild all the time without disciplining it, we can get off track and be led down a negative path. The good news for those who struggle with fear/worry/anxiety, is that you can make the effort and take the steps to renew your mind. It's scientifically possible! We have the science to prove it. But we don't do it alone! We have have the help of the Holy Spirit, to *"be transformed by the renewing of your mind,"* Romans 12:2. He knows that we can do it and now science has caught up in proving it. There *is* hope for you that you can make changes and rewire your brain and redirect your thoughts. You *can* start to heal from the painful past with the power of directing your thoughts to the positive and with prayer, the leadership of the Holy Spirit and discipline. You don't have to live in the cycle of worry and anxiety that you've been looping in. You can break free and begin to create new brain pathways that when practiced, will turn into brain highways of positive thoughts and courageous power!

God has given you the ability to do it. He will help you through this and transform your mind! Take the time to do the work and see the rewards that you will reap!

# Chapter 10

---

## Plan of Action

Any action worth taking, begins with a plan. The entire reason I began writing this book is that I felt God put it on my heart to share what I have learned with others. At the heart of who I am, one of the greatest ways I love to show love to others is by helping them. It's one of God's gifts to be a shepherd and desire to help others in any area possible. And at my core, I love to help. I want to help by sharing what God has revealed to me (I don't take credit for this, it's truly God's design, power of the Holy Spirit and that He's allowed me to be messenger).

I encourage you to take these next few pages very seriously. Implement them in your lives and don't wait until tomorrow to start. Make a decision right now to take a step of faith and be free from fear. Call out to God right now and ask Him to begin showing you the way out, and He *will*. You do your part, and God will do His part.

To begin, I want you to start with these simple steps. It's going to take some practice but we have the blessing of the Holy Spirit to help guide us so be encouraged that you're not doing this alone.

I call this first stage "The Warm up."

### The Warm-up steps:

1) be aware of what you're thinking about and if it's negative:

> -stop and start being aware of what you can be thankful for
>
> -change your mindset to the positive

2) Then pray and declare Scripture and affirmations (out loud, if possible).  *See examples on page 59/60

Continue these two steps all day long, each day with diligence. (The 'rinse and repeat' concept).

When I say 'think about what you're thinking about,' I'm referring to taking your thoughts captive. Being aware of what you're filling your mind with. Are you dwelling on past hurts and feelings? Are you dwelling on a painful situation or a fearful one? If you find that you are, make an effort to change that with the second step listed above.

That's the first part of the journey.

The next part of the journey involves some deeper insight and digging. You're going to want to really pray about where these fears have come from. The goal is to expose the truth and in doing so, exposing the lies. Lies lose their power when they're exposed and you can start to understand why you have those fears and worries, and begin to allow God to heal your heart and speak truth. When God exposed some of the lies that I was believing, and then told me the truth about who I am, I was a puddle of tears, but it was beautiful and happy, healthy tears. It was like a rock had been lifted off of my body and I could let that go and release it to God.

This part of the journey I call, "Digging Deeper"

### *Digging Deeper steps:*
3) make specific devotion time to pray and thank God, but also ask for some Holy Spirit counselling- really asking th Holy Spirit to reveal the root causes of your fears and worries.

4) make a list of the triggers, and start working through dealing with them (see example below, page 84, 85).

I am going to go into some detail about how to complete step 4 of the Digging Deeper steps. It takes a bit of explanation and examples.

### Digging Deeper Step 4- Chart

Begin by grabbing a notebook or some sheets of lined paper.

(For each area of fear/anxiety/worry, you will use a new piece of paper. You will reproduce the same outline for each page.)
On each page, write down the topic/area of fear. If you have 3 areas of fear (airplanes, finances and relationships), then you would write one heading on each page.

For each page, divide the paper into 3 columns.
Column 1: write **Triggers**
Column 2: write **What I'm Afraid of**
Column 3: write **What the Reality Is**

Let's discuss the columns in more detail and then you can begin the work.

### Triggers

This column is where you will write down the triggers in the area you're having anxiety. For example, if you're area of anxiety is health, you would write down triggers related to health like doctors visits, or getting sick or whatever your trigger is. The trigger is described as the antecedent that comes before the anxiety begins. It's the event that happens, that then *triggers* the anxiety/worry or fear. See example in the chart below.

### What I'm Afraid of

This column is where you will write down the worrisome thoughts that pass through your mind. This is where you get really honest with yourself about what's actually causing the fear. What are the exact thoughts you have run through your mind in that area? What things are you concerned about when that trigger happens? Be honest with yourself, even if it's painful or hard. Remember that you're doing the work so you can be free from the hamster wheel of worry that's going on in your mind. If you're not honest with yourself, you aren't going to be able to reach the clarity you need to proceed. You might write down only one thought surrounding your worry but I'm sure you have more than one thought pass through your mind when you're worrying about that issue, so write them all down. Even if you think they seem *way* out there or irrational, it doesn't matter. Write it down because writing it down releases the burden of keeping it cooped up in your mind, rolling around that hamster wheel. If you've thought it, write it, no matter how absurd it may sound at the time.

### What the reality is

When you're describing the reality, try to think of even if that does happen, what could be the outcome? It's not as if you're thinking worst case scenario, but instead you're thinking with a logical mind that if that thing does happen, you'll make it through, rather than building it up in our minds that we can't handle it. But you are stronger than you give yourself credit for. And on top of that, God is our strength when we have none (see 2 Corinthians 12:9-11). The reality is 99% of what we worry about will never happen. Think about that. And the other reality is that we worry that if that scenario *does* happen, we won't be able to handle it and that's what causes the worry and cycle of thinking the problem over in our mind, again and again, like clothes being rolled around in a dryer. They keep tumbling around and around, relentlessly. When you instead, face that problem directly on paper, you are taking the fear out of it and thinking about it from a logical place. You are bringing it into the light and allowing the Holy Spirit to speak truth into it. That removes the fear and and 'unknown' (which is mostly what we fear-the unknown) and allows you to bring it into the light, face it head on and pray about it and give it to God. When you look at it with logical eyes, you are taking the fear and the unknown factor out, and you can stop obsessing over it and rolling it around in your mind. That is the *freedom* I am speaking of. Being able to shut your mind off is in and of itself, freedom. It's as if you're actually turning the dryer cycle off, and just letting the clothes rest. Think about that…rest. Turning your mind off. That's what we struggle with, isn't it? Our mind is constantly swirling with ideas, fears, worries, projections, foretelling-so many things. And all of those things are out of our control. We cannot foresee or foretell the future yet we worry about it. We think that rolling it around in our mind a few hundred times will solve the problem but it doesn't! Because we are brought right back to the same starting point which is trying to predict the future. But we can't! And I would even add to that, that we take the joy out of the Father's heart when we don't rely on

Him. Remember, He is supposed to be our daily bread. Jehovah Jireh. Our provider. And when we try to predict the future and worry about our future, what we're in essence saying is that we trust ourselves to figure it out, more than Him.

But instead, when you being putting your trust in Him, giving these situations to God, praying over them and releasing your burdens, you are putting the reigns back in God's hands, where they are more safe and protected than anywhere else.

For each thought/point you wrote down under the "What I'm afraid of column," you must write the response to that thought under the "what the reality is" column. It will make more sense in the example below.

That's the idea behind this exercise and I encourage you to take the time to do this. I also encourage you to pray before you begin and let God do the revealing and listen to His still small voice, speaking to you. Speaking truth and light. After all, you're exposing this into the light, into God's hands and letting Him guide you. Giving Him your submission and your will, to bend it to His. Remember that we have a free will and God doesn't operate outside of that. Trusting Him to take care of us rather than our own agenda and will, is honouring to God. It allows Him to do a work in your life when you submit and surrender your will, worry, destiny, plans and fears, to Him.

Remember to make one sheet for each topic/area of worry.

See the example on the next page:

## Topic: Health

| Trigger… | What I'm afraid of… | What the reality is… |
|---|---|---|
| -visiting the hospital | a) I will pickup a sickness that will make me very sick<br>b) I won't be able to wait with all those sick people | a) I can pray for God's protection to not get sick and trust in Him.<br>And even if I do get sick, God is with me and will help me though it. There are trained nurses and doctors to help in any situation.<br>b) God is with me and I'm not alone. He will help me get through this and anything I encounter (repeat that to yourself) |
| -getting blood tests | a) that I will have bad results that could be serious | a) Trusting God and having faith for good results. And even though I trust Him, if the results aren't favourable I still trust God will work it out for my good by giving me the right doctors and options. |

Pray through these responses. Ask God to show you what he sees, what he says. Rely on Him to be your advocate and your responder.

Another example is on the next page.

## Topic: Travel

| Trigger... | What I'm afraid of... | What the reality is... |
|---|---|---|
| -getting on a plane | a) we could crash | a) Yes. The plane could crash. And I can't control that. And I know that God is in control and it's completely out of my control but I can pray and ask for God's favour and protection and trust in Him to take care of me. |
| -eating new foods in a new place | a) what if I have a reaction?<br>b) what if I get food poisoning?<br>c) I won't like the food in the new culture/place | a) There are trained staff to deal with these things. I can get through it with God's help, and there are doctors to help if necessary. I can instead pray over my food and trust in God to take care of me.<br>b) even if I don't love all the food, I know I can find something to have |

You'll notice a recurring theme here. Trust. I know for myself, I relied far too heavily on self-care, and I didn't even realize it. I was not putting my trust in God. For some reason I wanted to be in control of my circumstances and I realized through the leading of the Holy Spirit that it was because I was lacking trust. I wasn't trusting in God. At the root of it all, I had control issues with taking care of myself. Talk about a boat-load of pressure...who can have peace when you're relying on controlling things that are out of your control? In each situation, I can trust that God can do a good work in me. I can trust that He will take care of me, whether my worries are crowds, finances, travel, confrontation...it doesn't matter what the worry or the situation is, God can handle it and He works on our behalf to bring all things together for our good. (see Romans 8:28, John 14:13).

I also am reminded that even though I know that these scenarios are very unlikely to happen, writing them down is bringing it into the light. I can really give it to God to deal with. They're out of our control, and I had to get to a place of accepting that and then moving from acceptance to appreciation for what God can do when I give it to Him. We cannot go through life worrying about all the 'what ifs' because that is liable to make anyone sick with worry. Instead, we must trust in God that He's taking care of us like He promises in His Word (see Matthew 6:28) and I choose to surrender my will and my agenda, each day.

If I keep relying on myself to take care of these things, I am really stunting the ability God has to work on my behalf. He still works even when I'm not in submission but I believe that when we surrender our will, we are giving God abundance to work in, full-surrender of all our will. I know God doesn't operate out of our free will so we must submit our will to God in order for Him to work in and through us.

You really have to get to a place of surrender with this. know for me, it took a lot of time and prayer (*a lot* of prayer) to get to a place of truly trusting in God. It would have been easier if I had just trusted Him 100% from the start but I went through some things that really tested my faith (more about that later) to be honest. But I can truly look back and say that never once did God ever leave me in it. He walked me through each storm.

Once I got to the place of surrendering myself and my will and gave it all to Him, the worry and anxiety began to flee. And I encourage you to really do some soul-searching about your relationship with God and ask yourself how much you trust and rely on Him. You may not even realize that part of your anxiety is your attempt to control the things you cannot control. I know for me, control was a large part of the issue behind my anxiety. And I have to work at it now, to keep it in check and continually pray for God to renew my mind. And He does…He is faithful to the very end. So please take some time to evaluate your level of trust with the Lord. Ask yourself where you can trust Him more. I can almost guarantee that at least a few, if not all of your areas of anxiety, have to do with lack of trust in God, and reliance on self. It sounds harsh, I know, to think that we don't fully trust God. It sounds like we are blaming our anxiety/worry on that but when it really comes down to it, isn't that a huge part of what we are trying to control? Maybe for you, trust isn't an issue but it is another root, or more than one root. Pray and the Holy Spirit will show you.

I shared a few examples from my own personal struggles to show you that I struggled in my own journey with anxiety. But also to show you that these areas that I really used to battle with daily, are no longer a daily battle. As I mentioned earlier, I am not oblivious to the fact that I may still be tempted to worry once in a while, but I am aware of my struggle and I am able to submit it to God right away, as soon as I become aware. And being tempted to worry is different than giving into it! That is a *huge* part of the victory in this walk. The Holy Spirit reveals the truth to us and as it says right there in the Word of God, "The truth will set you free" (John 8:31). That has certainly been true for me. Taking these steps, and trusting God in these areas, being diligent and persevering, praying for God to transform my mind…all these things have been stepping stones on my path to freedom from worry and fear. I am no longer a marionette, being led by a string pulling me, from one direction to another, from one emotion to another, from one feeling to another. I am being led by the Holy Spirit and His guidance is not as fickle as a string. He lays a path before me, and I choose to walk upon it.

To summarize, the steps are as follows:

**The Warm-up steps:**

1) *be aware of what you're thinking about and if it's neg:*
>    *-stop and start being aware of what you can be thankful for*
>    *-change your mindset to the positive*

2) *Then pray and declare Scripture and affirmations out loud if possible (examples on page 59,60)*
*-continue this pattern all day long, each day with diligence. (The 'rinse and repeat' concept).*

**Digging Deeper steps:**

3) *make specific devotion time to pray and thank God, but also ask for some Holy Spirit counselling- really asking the Holy Spirit to reveal the root causes of your fears and worries*

4) *make a list of the triggers, and start working through dealing with them*

Each day you are one step closer than the day before. Remember what it says in 1 Corinthians 10:13, "Therefore we do not lose heart. Though outwardly we are wasting away, yet inwardly we are being renewed day by day." (NIV). We can hope and trust in the fact that God is taking us through this journey and that we are never alone. Don't look ahead at how far you have to go, but instead be proud of how far you've come, each day…one step at a time. Rome wasn't built in a day. It takes a *day by day* approach and mindset. Set your mind on things above and let the Holy Spirit do the work He will do in, and through you.

# Chapter 11

---

## Forging Forward

You are well on your way to conquering fear! You have learned some truths from the Word of God and some practical steps to implement in your daily walk. You've learned about:

- the power of thoughts
- the power of the Holy Spirit's guidance
- healing from the past
- exposing the truth
- the importance of gratitude and peace
- neuroplasticity
- the plan of action you can implement

All of these tools will help you in the journey you're on. I am proud of you for taking the time to invest in yourself and your happiness. I believe that you want to see change and God is giving you the tools to help you begin to walk in freedom. I believe that freedom is a core desire for everyone. Not everyone will achieve freedom here on earth but I believe we all desire it. God wants you to be free.

*"Now the Lord is the Spirit, and where the Spirit of the Lord is, there is **freedom**." 2 Corinthians 3:17 (NIV, emphasis mine).*

*"So if the Son sets you **free**, you will be free indeed." John 8:36 (NIV, emphasis mine).*

He wants to see you living a life that's exciting, joyful, enjoyable and free. Living in a state of worry and fear creates anxiety and holds you back from your true potential. It holds your family and loved ones back. You don't want to live this way anymore and today is the first day of your new life. Today is the first day where you take a step forward. It's the day you begin to take back the ground that the enemy has taken from you:

*"Instead of your shame you will receive a **double portion**, and instead of disgrace you will rejoice in your inheritance. And so you will inherit a **double portion** in your land, and everlasting joy will be yours." Isaiah 61:7 (emphasis mine)*

Today is the day you stand up and say, "No more fear. No more panic. No more living in the past. I am looking forward to the future and my future is bright. I am going to do this. I *can* do this. God is with me and if He is for me, then who can be against me (Romans 8:31). No weapon formed against me will prosper (Isaiah 54:17)."

We are not in charge. Yes, we choose whether we follow God or not. We have choice in what path we want to walk down. But ultimately, God is in charge whether we acknowledge that or not. If you're running away from wanting to face these issues, God will find a way to continue to show you to work on this. He won't give up on you. He won't leave you in the mess you're in. He will gently prompt you many times, but at some point, God will make it clear that it's time to work on it. It could be through more obvious circumstances or it could be through an encouragement of a friend. Either way, don't ignore His calling to you. There's a reason you decided to read this book. There's a reason you were led to begin this journey. He's calling to you, to trust Him and let Him help you through this. After all, who better to lead you through this? He's the shepherd who longs to take care of His sheep. He will leave the 99 to go after the one and make sure that sheep is safe (see Matthew 18:12-14). That one sheep…is you. And He cannot wait to set you free through this journey. Trust in Him. In the middle of the practicing and setting your mind to continue on, know that you are not doing it alone and He will help you. The first leg of the journey is step by step, methodical and the hardest part, but as you continue on you will see that it gets easier and easier. Those muscles begin to grow and build up and before long, what used to be hard is now second-nature. You are now not just slowly stammering down the path but you are running, leaping over obstacles and rushing forward into the new life that God has for you. Embrace it and know that with each of those steps, He's there.

Continue to practice being aware of your thoughts. This isn't a one-time solution. It does take diligence and persistence. Some areas may always be harder to overcome than others but that doesn't mean you should to give up. It does get easier. Even the areas that were once very hard for me to overcome, are now much easier than when I first began. I have far more victory than ever before and if I do begin to feel my mind drifting towards the past or astray, I quickly practice praying out loud, speaking the Word of God out loud and keeping my mind on the positive. God has always been faithful to help me along and He will be faithful to you as well. If you slip up and feel you've gone backwards, don't be afraid. It means the enemy is testing you by trying to tempt you, and trying to get you to think it's not working but don't believe his lies. He's not very inventive as he uses that same lie on anyone who's trying to get out of addiction. And in many ways, getting in the pattern of worry and fear is like addiction in the sense that you get stuck in the pattern of it and you need to practice overcoming it. Alcoholics purpose each day to be in charge of their actions and not pick up a drink. The temptation is still there-stronger some days than others-but like with anything, the more you practice, the easier it gets. And the same goes for taking these thoughts captive. The more you practice, the easier it gets.

If you keep feeling defeated or feel that you're getting tempted to slip back into old patterns, pray and fight the enemy with the Word and let God fight the battles for you. Know that you **can** do it and that the enemy is lying to you. God is your Vindicator and He **will** fight for you.

One last thought I want to share with you that is a new revelation to me, but one that has really increased my faith and victory. It's something God revealed to me a number of months ago and as I've been walking it out, I see exactly why God showed me this. Because it's effective and it keeps breeding more and more faith. It's about the power and purpose of faith.

Our faith can move mountains. Think about that for a moment. It says in Matthew 17:20 : *"And He said to them, "Because of the littleness of your faith; for truly I say to you, if you have faith the size of a mustard seed, you will say to this mountain, 'Move from here to there,' and it will move; and nothing will be impossible to you."* (also see Mark 11:23). In fact, I read in Bill Johnson's testimony (the pastor of the mega-church Bethel, in Redding, California), that when he was pursuing a deeper relationship with God, he was praying so heavily and deeply for the presence of God. He was seeking God's presence with all his heart. He would find himself waking up in prayer, asking for more of

God. He says he was obsessed-he wanted to see more of God and know Him more deeply. One night, he was awoken at 3am. All of the sudden, his entire body was electric and full of this strong energy. It was so powerful that he could not move. He could not speak. He said it was so strong that he was almost afraid, yet at the same time, he knew it was God and felt a sense of peace. It lasted for 3 hours and then it went away. This happened for 3 nights in a row and it changed him. He was suddenly struck, in awe, of the presence of God. He was amazed at the power of His Mighty Hand. He knew that God could do absolutely anything. (see "The Essential Guide to Healing" by Bill Johnson and Randy Clark, for this testimony).

The power of just *reading* that testimony spoke the exact same thing to me. Although I didn't physically experience what Bill did, in hearing his testimony I was impacted by the awe-some power of God. That God could do absolutely anything and we are powerless to stop it. He is in control. He can move an actual mountain. He can turn day to night and night to day. His power is immense and yet we are so quick to put Him in a little comfy box that we are comfortable with.

God has given us the measure of faith we need, it says in Romans 12:3. And when I connect that to the above verse in Matthew about our faith moving mountains, I am reminded that if our faith can do that, then having faith for freedom from anxiety is a drop in the bucket.

Suffice to say with all of that, that the truth that God revealed to me was this: ***in God's economy, faith goes first and then comes the results.*** If I have faith and truly believe in God's working power, truly believe that I can overcome, God shows up and works miracles. I continue to trust Him and even if I don't see the results yet, I keep hoping on in faith and God uses that faith to move mountains. God is at work, even when we don't see or feel it and when we hold strong in our faith He continues to work and build us up. Don't let go of your faith that you can do this! Don't let go of your faith that God is going to show you the way out. Keep holding on above anything else you think or feel because faith goes first, and results follow after.

An example of this is the story of Daniel. We read in Daniel 10:13 that Daniel was praying to God and asking Him to send help. As he prayed, he didn't see anything happening but he kept praying and hoping on in faith. It says he prayed diligently for 21 days and did not yet see a result. An angel came to him on day 21 and the angel said that he was sent earlier but the prince of darkness was in his way and he could not come and help Daniel. For 21 days the angel kept trying to fight this darkness. He the angel called upon a stronger angel, Michael, who is a warrior angel. Michael defeated the prince of darkness and the first angel was able to proceed to Daniel. We can infer from this, that if Daniel had stopped praying, the angel wouldn't have made it there. He had to keep praying and hoping on in faith and we must do the same. Daniel didn't see the results of his prayers for 21 days, yet he kept on trusting and praying.

Be encouraged that you may not feel it's easy the first few days. You may not feel or see the results immediately but trust that if you keep hoping on in faith (1 Timothy 6:12) and stay strong in your faith to trust that God *is* at work and will see you through this, you will be rewarded. Fight the good fight of faith and see God's faithfulness poured out upon you! See the chains fall off and walk in the freedom He brings! I'll say it again: *YOU CAN DO THIS!* God is on your side and He is there to fight the battles for you and see you walk into victory!

All it takes is the first step.

## About the Author

Chelsey Dollman is a passionate writer, who lives in the heart of the Cowichan Valley, and whose desire is to see people set free, be encouraged and live a life of freedom. She has a B.A and B.Ed, and enjoys teaching in many varied capacities. She now spends her time with her children and husband, hiking trails and seeing the beauty of God in the creation around her. This is her first published book, and she hopes it is the first of many.

# Works Cited

"Emotional Memories Function In Self-Reinforcing Loop." ScienceDaily, ScienceDaily, 24 Mar. 2005, www.sciencedaily.com/releases/ 2005/03/050323130625.htm.

Holy Bible: New Living Translation. Wheaton, Ill: Tyndale House Publishers, 2004. Print.

Meyer, Joyce. Battlefield Of The Mind: How To Win The War In Your Mind. Tulsa, Okla. : Harrison House, 1995.

"Peace (in the Bible)." New Catholic Encyclopedia, Encyclopedia.com, 30 Mar. 2020, www.encyclopedia.com/ religion/encyclopedias-almanacs-transcripts-and-maps/ peace-bible.

"Peace." Merriam-Webster, Merriam-Webster, www.merriam-webster.com/dictionary/peace.

The Holy Bible, New International Version. Grand Rapids: Zondervan House, 1984. Print.

Manufactured by Amazon.ca
Bolton, ON